MW01243824

For My Boys

Patty E. Parker

Dallas, Texas

By
Patty E. Parker

Cover art and illustrations by Missy Murphey.

Additional copies of **For My Boys** may be obtained at the cost of $14.95, plus $3.00 postage and handling, each book. Texas residents add $1.23 sales tax, each book.

Send to:

A Cerf In The Kitchen
8409 Pickwick Ln. #182
Dallas, Texas 75225

Copyright © 1997
A Cerf In The Kitchen
Dallas, Texas

ISBN 0-9659989-0-8

First Printing October, 1997

Printed in the USA by

WIMMER
The Wimmer Companies
Memphis

July 15, 1997

Dear Chris and Charlie,

Well, here it is. I know you both thought that the infamous cookbook would never be a reality and yet, you now have it in your hands. It is with great pride that I dedicate it to you both. You have been more than patient with me in the countless hours spent organizing, imputing, and even testing to produce **For My Boys**. I hope that as you grow older, this book will be a keepsake and a remembrance of all our family and friends that helped it come to fruition. Both of your grandmothers are ever present in this book and are simply listed as *Mom* and as *Vers*. Each had a significant impact on my culinary abilities, and I hope that you will benefit as well. Our friends are also remembered within these pages. They shared their favorite recipes, and many also shared their time and efforts in helping me complete this project. Susie, Anne, Marti, and your Aunt Kathy were integral parts. They spent many hours helping me complete a long awaited goal.

You are the loves of my life. The joy you bring to me is the greatest of gifts. I will treasure you both forever.

All My Love,

Mom

ACKNOWLEDGMENTS

There are not enough words to adequately thank all who have contributed to the completion of this cookbook. I am grateful to those who allowed me the use of their recipes. To Sue Geren, Anne Duke, and Marti Clinesmith, I thank you for all your patience in imputing, editing, and recipe consideration. To Missy Murphey, I am indebted for your beautiful work on the division pages as well as the cover. I am honored to be the recipient of your first published works. And finally, to my sister Kathy for her constant support and understanding and to my Mother whom I hope I may emulate for the rest of my life.

Patty

TABLE OF CONTENTS

Introduction   3

Acknowledgments   4

Appetizers   8

Beverages   31

Soups   34

Salads   39

Brunch   54

Breads   67

Vegetables   78

Entrées   102

Desserts   142

Index   179

Appetizers

ARTICHOKE DIP

1 14-ounce can artichoke
   hearts, drained and
   chopped
1 cup mayonnaise
1 cup grated Parmesan
   cheese

Mix all of the above and place in a small shallow baking dish. Bake at 350° until bubbly. Serve with crackers.

ARTICHOKE NIBBLES

2 6-ounce jars marinated
   artichoke hearts
1 small onion, finely
   chopped
1 clove garlic, minced
¼ cup fine dried bread
   crumbs
4 eggs, beaten
¼ teaspoon salt
⅛ teaspoon pepper
⅛ teaspoon oregano
⅛ teaspoon hot sauce
8 ounces grated sharp
   Cheddar cheese
2 tablespoons chopped
   parsley

Drain artichokes, retain marinade from one jar. Chop artichokes. Place marinade liquid in a skillet and sauté onions and garlic. Drain excess marinade. Add bread crumbs and seasoning to eggs. Stir in cheese, parsley, onion mixture and artichokes. Bake in a greased 7x11-inch pan at 325° for 30 minutes. May be served hot or cold.

ARTICHOKE & SHRIMP DIP

1 14-ounce can artichoke
   hearts, drained
1 4½-ounce can shrimp,
   rinsed and drained
1 3-ounce package cream
   cheese, softened
½ cup mayonnaise
½ cup salsa
¼ cup grated Parmesan
   cheese

Dice artichoke hearts. Add all other ingredients and mix well. Spoon into a 9-inch round pie plate. Bake at 350° about 20 minutes or until heated through. Serve with crackers or chips.

HOT BLACK-EYED PEA DIP

2   5-ounce jars Old English cheese
½   cup butter
½   medium onion, chopped
2   15-ounce cans black-eyed peas
3   jalapeño peppers, seeded and diced
1   4-ounce can chopped green chilies
Garlic salt

Melt cheese over low heat. In a skillet, melt butter and sauté onions until soft. Drain peas and add to melted cheese. Add onions, jalapeños, chilies and garlic salt to taste. Mix well and serve hot with corn chips.

BLACK-EYED PEA DIP

2   cans black-eyed peas
1   stick margarine
1   6-ounce roll jalapeño cheese
1   6-ounce roll garlic cheese
1   medium onion, chopped
4   cloves garlic, minced
2   tablespoons jalapeño, seeded and chopped

Sauté onion, garlic and jalapeño in margarine until wilted. Add cheeses and black-eyed peas and heat until melted, stirring often to prevent sticking. Serve in chafing dish with tortilla or corn chips.

TOASTED BRIE

1   small round of Brie
½   cup brown sugar
1   teaspoon dry mustard
½   cup slivered almonds
White wine

Place Brie on oven proof dish. Mix brown sugar and mustard with enough white wine until consistency of peanut butter. Spread on top of Brie and top with almonds. Broil on lowest oven rack until sugar bubbles (about 3 minutes). Watch carefully.

Carolyn B. Wallace

9

BOB'S DIP

1 cup spicy refried bean dip, canned
¼ cup medium picante sauce
¼ teaspoon cumin
¼ teaspoon chili powder
Velveeta cheese
Guacamole
1 cup sour cream

Mix bean dip, picante sauce, cumin and chili powder. Spread on the bottom of and ovenproof dish. Cover the beans with ¼-inch thick slices of Velveeta. Top cheese layer with guacamole. Spread sour cream over guacamole. Bake at 350° for 20 minutes or until bubbly. Serve with tortilla chips.

Kathy Daume

BACON BREAD

6 slices bacon, cooked and crumbled
1 cup grated Cheddar cheese
2 tablespoons minced green onions
¼ teaspoon Worcestershire
¼ cup Miracle Whip
1 loaf party rye bread slices

Mix first five ingredients and spread on rye bread slices. Broil until bubbly. Serve hot. May add chopped mushrooms for added flavor.

Marti Clinesmith

HOT BREAD SNACKS

2 cups sharp Cheddar cheese, grated
1 cup mayonnaise
1 small can chopped black olives
1 bunch green onions, chopped
1 teaspoon curry powder
1 teaspoon black pepper
¾ teaspoon salt
1 package English muffins, split

Mix first seven ingredients and spread on English muffin halves. Bake at 375° for 10 to 15 minutes or until bubbly. Cut into quarters and serve warm.

Marti Clinesmith

FRENCH BREAD SPREAD

1 small can chopped
   black olives
½ stick melted butter
2 cups Mozzarella cheese,
   grated
¾ cup mayonnaise
1 teaspoon garlic powder
1 large loaf French bread

Mix all ingredients and spread on French bread halves. Bake at 350° until cheese melts then broil until lightly browned. Can be sliced before baked.

Sue Geren

HOT CHEESE CANAPÉS

16 white bread rounds
½   pound chopped, cooked
    shrimp or crab meat
½   cup mayonnaise
1   cup finely grated
    Cheddar cheese
2   chopped green onions
Dash of Worcestershire
Dash of Tabasco

Toast bread rounds on both sides in oven. Combine all other ingredients and spread on toasted rounds. Broil about 4 inches from heat until bubbly and browned.

Mable Cook

CHILI DIP

1 pound ground beef
2 medium onions,
   chopped
2 cans chili beef soup
2 cans Rotel diced
   tomatoes
2 8-ounce cans tomato
   sauce
2 cans refried beans
2 cups grated Cheddar
   cheese
4 green onions, chopped

Brown meat and onion and drain. Add soup, Rotel, tomato sauce and beans. Stir and simmer 15 minutes. Before serving, top with cheese and green onions. Serve with chips.

Nancy Kendzior

BROCCOLI DIP

2   10-ounce packages frozen chopped broccoli
1   6-ounce roll garlic cheese, cut into cubes
1   tablespoon butter
1   small onion, chopped
1   4.5-ounce jar sliced mushrooms, drained
1½ cans cream of mushroom soup

Cook broccoli according to package directions. Drain. In a skillet, sauté onions and mushrooms in butter and add to broccoli. Stir in cheese and soup and cook over low heat until cheese is melted. Serve immediately with corn chips.

CRABMEAT MORNAY DIP

1   stick butter
1   small bunch green onions, chopped
½   cup finely chopped parsley
2   tablespoons flour
1   pint half-and-half
½   pound Swiss cheese, grated
1   tablespoon sherry
Red pepper
Salt
1   pound jumbo lump crabmeat

Melt butter in heavy pot and sauté onions and parsley. Blend in flour, cream and cheese and heat until cheese is melted, stirring constantly. Add other ingredients, seasoning with red pepper and salt to taste. Gently fold in crabmeat. Serve hot with small Melba toast rounds.

Sue Geren

HOT CRABMEAT CHEESE PUFFS

½ pound crabmeat
4 green onions, chopped
½ cup grated Monterey Jack cheese
½ cup grated Cheddar cheese
½ cup mayonnaise
1 teaspoon lemon juice
¼ teaspoon curry powder
1 10-ounce package flaky-style refrigerator biscuits

Combine all ingredients, except rolls, and mix well. Separate each roll into 3 layers. Place on ungreased cookie sheet and spread crabmeat mixture on top of each biscuit layer. Bake at 400° for about 10 minutes or until golden brown.

CRAB-STUFFED MUSHROOMS

¾ pound large mushrooms
1 8-ounce package cream cheese, softened
½ cup finely crushed croutons
¼ teaspoon garlic powder
½ pound crab meat
2 tablespoons grated Parmesan cheese
Paprika

Remove stems from mushrooms and wash well. Pat dry with a paper towel. Mix cream cheese, croutons and garlic powder until well blended. Stir crab into cream cheese. Fill each mushroom cap with crab meat mixture. Sprinkle with paprika. Place on a baking sheet and broil until bubbling hot, about 5 minutes.

JALAPEÑO CHEESE SQUARES

4 cups (16-ounces) shredded Cheddar cheese
4 eggs, beaten
1 teaspoon minced onion
4 small cans jalapeño peppers, drained, seeded and chopped

Combine all ingredients and mix well. Spread in an ungreased 8-inch square pan. Bake at 350° for 30 minutes. To serve, cut into squares.

Marti Clinesmith

SHRIMP CON QUESO

1   32-ounce package
    Velveeta cheese
1   8-ounce cream cheese
1   10¾-ounce can cream of
    shrimp soup
2   can Rotel tomatoes
½   cup finely chopped
    onion
1   teaspoon minced garlic
2   tablespoons butter or
    margarine
2   tablespoons cumin seed
1   teaspoon basil
½   teaspoon sugar
2   tablespoons
    Worcestershire
1   pound cooked shrimp,
    peeled and cut into bite
    size pieces

Combine all ingredients except shrimp in a large double boiler. Heat over hot water, stirring frequently, until cheese is melted and mixture is well blended. Add shrimp to mixture and heat thoroughly. Serve in chafing dish with tortilla or corn chips.

May be frozen for up to six weeks.

Makes 11 cups

Sue Geren

HOT ONION DIP

1   12-ounce package
    frozen chopped onions
3   cups grated Swiss
    cheese
1   cup mayonnaise
1   tablespoon coarse
    Dijon mustard

Thaw onions and remove excess moisture with a paper towel. Combine all ingredients and bake at 325° for 25 minutes. Serve hot with crackers.

EASY STUFFED MUSHROOMS

½ pound medium sized mushrooms
4 ounces Swiss cheese, grated
1 hard-boiled egg, finely chopped
4 tablespoons seasoned dry bread crumbs
4 tablespoons butter, softened

Remove stems from mushrooms and clean caps. Mix remaining ingredients and stuff mushroom caps, mounding the filling over caps. Place in a lightly buttered casserole with sides touching. Bake at 350° for 15 to 20 minutes. Serve warm.

MUSHROOM CRESCENT SNACKS

3 cups finely chopped fresh mushrooms
2 tablespoons butter, melted
1 teaspoon garlic powder
1 teaspoon finely chopped onion
1 teaspoon lemon juice
1 teaspoon Worcestershire sauce
1 8-ounce can refrigerated crescent rolls
1 3-ounce package cream cheese, softened
¼ cup grated Parmesan cheese

Brown mushrooms in butter. Add garlic powder, onion, lemon juice, and Worcestershire sauce. Stir and cook until liquid evaporates. Set aside. Separate dough into 2 long rectangles. Place in an ungreased 9x13-inch pan; press over bottom and ¼ inch up sides to form crust. Spread cream cheese over dough. Top with mushroom mixture and sprinkle with Parmesan cheese. Bake at 350° for 20 to 25 minutes or until golden brown. Cool 5 minutes, then cut into desired shapes. Serve warm.

Yields 24

PARMESAN MUSTARD CHICKEN WINGS

1   stick unsalted butter, melted
2   tablespoons Dijon mustard
½   teaspoon cayenne pepper
1   cup dry bread crumbs
½   cup freshly grated Parmesan cheese
1   teaspoon ground cumin
Salt and pepper
20 chicken wings

In a shallow dish, whisk together butter, mustard, and cayenne. In another shallow dish, combine bread crumbs, cheese, cumin and salt and pepper to taste. Dip chicken in butter mixture and then coat with crumbs. Arrange without touching on a greased baking pan. Bake in lower part of oven at 425° for 30 minutes. Can be turned after 20 minutes for extra crispness.

Serves 6

Jean Finch

PARTY PIZZAS

1   pound bulk pork sausage
1   pound ground beef
2   tablespoons oregano
½   teaspoon garlic salt
½   teaspoon Worcestershire sauce
1   pound Velveeta, cubed
2   loaves party rye

Brown sausage and beef in a skillet. Drain well. Add remaining ingredients except bread. Heat until cheese melts, stirring often. Spread on rye slices. Freeze on cookie sheet, then place in plastic bags and keep in freezer until ready to serve. Bake as needed at 400° for 10 minutes or until bubbly.

Sue Geren

SPINACH ARTICHOKE DIP

1   stick butter
2   10-ounce packages
    frozen chopped spinach
1   large can artichoke
    hearts, drained and
    chopped
1   8-ounce carton sour
    cream
½   cup onion, chopped
½   cup grated Parmesan
    cheese
Salt and pepper to taste

Cook spinach according to package directions. Drain well. Sauté onions in butter. Mix all ingredients and heat through. Serve warm in deep casserole dish or chafing dish.

HOT PARMESAN SPINACH DIP

1   onion, chopped
1   clove garlic, minced
1   package frozen
    chopped spinach,
    thawed and squeezed
    dry
1⅓ cups grated Parmesan
    cheese
4   ounces cream cheese,
    softened
1   cup mayonnaise
Cayenne pepper
Black pepper

Mix all ingredients and spread in a greased shallow baking dish. Sprinkle additional cheese on top and more cayenne pepper if desired. Bake at 300° for approximately 20 minutes or until hot.

Nancy Kendzior

17

Tomato Toasties

½ teaspoon salt
½ cup grated mild Cheddar cheese
½ cup mayonnaise
¼ cup chopped green onion
½ pound bacon, cooked and crumbled
1 pint cherry tomatoes, sliced
French style rolls

Combine first 5 ingredients. Slice rolls about ¼-inch thick and then cut in half. Spread a little mayonnaise on each slice of bread. Place a slice of tomato on each and then 1 teaspoon of mixture on top of tomato. Broil until lightly browned.

Makes about 3½ dozen

Almond Cheese Spread

2 cups sharp Cheddar cheese, grated
1 green onion, chopped
4 slices bacon, cooked and crumbled
1 cup mayonnaise
1 2½-ounce package sliced almonds

Mix all of the above ingredients together. May be made the night before. Refrigerate until ready to serve. Serve with crackers.

Cheese Ring

1 pound sharp Cheddar cheese, grated
1 cup pecans, chopped
¾ cup mayonnaise
1 small onion, grated
1 clove garlic, pressed
½ teaspoon red pepper sauce
1 cup strawberry preserves

Combine all ingredients except preserves and mix well. Lightly grease a small mold with mayonnaise and add mixture. Chill for several hours. Just before serving, empty mold onto a plate or tray and fill the inside with strawberry preserves. Serve with crackers.

ARTICHOKE BACON DIP

1   14-ounce can artichoke
    hearts
½   cup mayonnaise
1   teaspoon
    Worcestershire sauce
2   teaspoons grated onion
3   slices bacon, cooked
    and crumbled
Red pepper

Drain artichoke hearts and then mash with a fork. Combine remaining ingredients and add mashed artichoke hearts. Chill for several hours. Before serving, sprinkle with red pepper. Serve with crackers.

COLD ARTICHOKE DIP

1   cup mayonnaise
1   package Good Seasons
    Italian Salad Dressing
    mix
2   cans artichoke hearts,
    drained and chopped
¾   cup grated Parmesan
    cheese
Dash of Tabasco sauce

Combine mayonnaise and Italian dressing until well blended. Add remaining ingredients and refrigerate several hours before serving. May even be made the night before serving. Serve with crackers.

Frances Templeton

COLD ARTICHOKE SPREAD

1   can artichoke hearts,
    drained
1   package dry ranch
    dressing mix
1   8-ounce carton sour
    cream
3   tablespoons
    mayonnaise
Tabasco sauce

In a medium mixing bowl, combine sour cream, mayonnaise, and ranch dressing. Mix thoroughly. Add artichokes and mix thoroughly. Cover and chill until ready to serve. Serve with crackers.

19

BACON AND TOMATO SPREAD

1   8-ounce package cream
    cheese, softened
2   teaspoons prepared
    mustard
½   teaspoon garlic salt
6   slices bacon, cooked
    crisp, drained and
    crumbled
1   medium, ripe tomato,
    peeled, seeded, drained,
    and finely chopped
¼   cup finely chopped
    green pepper

Combine cream cheese, mustard and garlic salt. Add bacon, tomato, and green pepper. Cover and chill for several hours. Serve with bagel crisps or melba toast.

BACON CHEESE SPREAD

1   pound sharp Cheddar
    cheese, grated
16 pieces bacon, cooked
    crisp, drained and
    crumbled
12 green onion, chopped
1   cup toasted slivered
    almonds
1   cup mayonnaise

Combine all ingredients. Add additional mayonnaise if needed. Refrigerate. Serve with crackers.

CHEESE SPREAD

10 ounces Cheddar cheese,
    grated
10 ounces butter, softened
2   tablespoons sherry
1   tablespoon horseradish
½   teaspoon garlic salt

Combine all ingredients and refrigerate for several hours. Serve with crackers.

CHUTNEY CHEESE SPREAD

6   ounces cream cheese, softened
8   ounces grated Cheddar cheese
2   tablespoons sherry
½   teaspoon curry powder
Mango chutney
Chives

Mix first four ingredients together until well blended. Spread on plate or tray. Top with mango chutney and chives. Serve with crackers.

CURRIED CHUTNEY SPREAD

2   8-ounce packages cream cheese, softened
½   cup chutney
½   cup toasted chopped almonds
1   teaspoon curry powder
½   teaspoon dry mustard

Combine all ingredients. Refrigerate for several hours. Serve with crackers.

EASY CLAM DIP

1   6¾-ounce can minced clams
1   8-ounce package cream cheese, softened
¼   teaspoon salt
2   teaspoons grated onion
1   teaspoon Worcestershire sauce
3   drops Tabasco
2   teaspoons lemon juice
1   teaspoon chopped parsley

Drain clams, reserving the liquid. Combine all ingredients except clam juice and blend. Gradually add about ¼ cup of the juice and beat. Chill before serving. Serve with crackers.

CLAM DIP

1   6½-ounce can minced clams, drain and save liquid
2   teaspoons prepared horseradish
1   3-ounce package cream cheese, softened
1   teaspoon lemon juice
1   teaspoon Worcestershire sauce

Mix horseradish, 1 teaspoon clam juice, Worcestershire sauce and lemon juice with cream cheese. Add clams with enough clam juice for desired consistency. Serve with chips or raw vegetables.

CRAB DIP

2   8-ounce packages cream cheese, softened
¼   cup mayonnaise
1   tablespoon lemon juice
1   tablespoon minced onion
1   teaspoon garlic salt
1   can white lump crab meat, drained
1   jar red cocktail sauce
Lemon
Parsley flakes
Wheat Thins

Mix first five ingredients and spread on a platter. Should be about 1-inch thick. Top with crab and the juice of half a lemon and then enough cocktail sauce to cover. Sprinkle with parsley flakes. Serve cold with crackers.

CRAB TORTILLA ROLLUPS

6   flour tortillas
1   pint spicy Cajun crab dip (buy in the deli)
2   green onions, chopped
¼   cup pecan pieces

Mix crab dip, green onions and pecans. Spread on tortillas and roll up, jelly roll style. Refrigerate, covered until ready to serve. Slice into 1-inch pieces and serve.

Sue Geren

CRABMEAT DIP

1 stick butter
1 small onion, chopped fine
1 pound crabmeat, picked clean
1 8-ounce package cream cheese
Dash of black pepper
Dash of Tabasco

Sauté onion in butter until tender. Add cream cheese. Mix well and cook over low heat until cheese is melted. Add crabmeat, pepper and Tabasco. Stir until heated through and creamy. Serve immediately with crackers.

Aline Murphey

JALAPEÑO DEVILED EGGS

6 eggs
1 large can jalapeños
3 tablespoons mayonnaise
1 teaspoon prepared mustard
½ teaspoon garlic salt
½ teaspoon onion powder
⅛ teaspoon pepper
⅛ teaspoon Worcestershire sauce

Place eggs in a saucepan and cover with cold water. Bring eggs to a boil and continue cooking for fifteen minutes. Peel eggs and allow to cool. Place eggs in a large jar and cover with jalapeños and juice. Store in refrigerator for at least five days. When ready to serve, remove eggs and slice in half. Put the yolks in a small mixing bowl. Mash yolks and add all other ingredients. Fill each egg white with yolk mixture and either serve immediately or refrigerate.

Eggs may be left in jalapeño mixture for an indefinite amount of time before deviling.

Makes a dozen deviled eggs

23

DEVILED EGGS

6 eggs
3 tablespoons mayonnaise
1 teaspoon prepared mustard
½ teaspoon garlic salt
½ teaspoon onion powder
⅛ teaspoon pepper
⅛ teaspoon Worcestershire sauce

Place eggs in a saucepan and cover with cold water. Bring to a boil. Continue boiling eggs for fifteen minutes. Peel eggs and allow to cool. Slice eggs in half and place yolks in a small mixing bowl. Mash yolks and add all other ingredients. Fill each egg white with yolk mixture and either serve immediately or refrigerate.

Makes a dozen deviled eggs

JALAPEÑO DIP

2 pounds Velveeta cheese, softened
1 pint Miracle Whip
1 onion, peeled and cut into pieces
½ 7-ounce can jalapeños with juice
1 clove garlic, chopped

In a blender mix onion, jalapeño and garlic. Add cheese and miracle whip. Serve with chips or raw vegetables.

Freezes well.

Makes 2 quarts

Kathy Daume

GUATEMALAN GUACAMOLE

4 ripe avocados
⅓ cup chopped onion
2 lemons, juiced
½ teaspoon oregano, optional

In a mixing bowl, mash avocados. Add the onions. Stir in lemon juice, salt and oregano. Serve immediately or store in refrigerator. Place avocado pit in dip to keep from turning brown.

Martha Cifuentes

EASY GUACAMOLE

4 ripe avocados
1 can Herdes Salsa
Caserra
Juice of ½ lemon
Salt
Pepper

Mash avocados and add all other ingredients. If made ahead of serving time, place pit of avocado in mixture to keep from turning brown.

Charlie Geren

GREEN CHILIE AND CHEESE DIP

1 8-ounce package cream cheese, softened
1½ cups Cheddar cheese, shredded
1 tablespoon lemon juice
1 tablespoon chicken-flavored bouillon granules
Dash of Tabasco
1 medium tomato, chopped
1 4.5-ounce can chopped green chilies, drained
1 tablespoon finely chopped onion

Combine cream cheese, Cheddar cheese, lemon juice, bouillon and Tabasco and beat at medium speed with an electric mixer until smooth. Gently stir in tomatoes, green chilies and onion. Refrigerate until ready to serve.

EVERYONE'S FAVORITE DIP

1 8-ounce carton sour cream
1 package Good Seasons Italian Salad Dressing Mix
1 tablespoon mayonnaise
½ avocado, chopped
Juice of ½ lemon
½ tomato, chopped
Dash of Tabasco

Combine sour cream, dressing mix and mayonnaise and mix well. Add vegetables. Sprinkle lemon juice over avocados. Add Tabasco and blend. Refrigerate. Serve with corn chips.

MANGO SALSA

2 cups diced tomatoes

1 jar sliced mango (on ice in deli-case), diced

1 bell pepper, seeded and diced

1 bunch green onions, diced

2 large jalapeños, seeded and minced

¼ cup lime juice

½ cup fresh cilantro, minced, optional

½ cup pecan pieces

Combine all ingredients. Serve cold with chips, steaks, chicken or pork.

Kathy Daume

PINEAPPLE SALSA

1 8-ounce can crushed pineapple, drained

2 tablespoons orange marmalade

1 tablespoon cilantro, chopped

2 teaspoons jalapeño, seeded and finely chopped

2 teaspoons lime juice

¼ teaspoon salt

Mix all ingredients until well blended. Cover and refrigerate until ready to serve. Serve with chips or as an accompaniment to chicken, pork or fish.

Yields 1 cup

MEXICAN LAYER DIP

1   can jalapeño bean dip
1   8-ounce carton sour
     cream
1   medium tomato, diced
1   avocado, diced
½   small can chopped
     black olives
Garlic salt
Picante sauce
Grated Cheddar cheese

In a pie plate or quiche dish, layer ingredients as listed. Picante sauce is to taste. End with cheese. Serve with chips.

MEXICAN LAYER DIP II

1   8-ounce package cream
     cheese, softened
1   tablespoon taco
     seasoning mix
1   avocado, diced
1   cup salsa
½   cup chopped green
     onions
½   small can chopped
     black olives
1   cup grated Cheddar
     cheese

Combine softened cream cheese and taco seasoning. Spread on the bottom of a pie plate or quiche dish. Layer remaining ingredients over cream cheese mixture, ending with cheese. Refrigerate. Serve with chips.

OYSTER CRACKER SNACK

1 package oyster crackers
1 cup oil
1 package Hidden Valley Ranch Dressing Mix (dry)
1 teaspoon garlic powder
1 teaspoon dill weed
1 teaspoon onion powder
1 cup chopped nuts, optional

In a large mixing bowl, combine all dry ingredients together. Add oil slowly while stirring mixture. Stir well every 15 minutes for 1 hour. Add chopped nuts if desired.

Sylvia Johnson

FRESH SHRIMP DIP

1 pound shrimp, cooked and diced
1½ cups mayonnaise
¼ cup chopped fresh parsley
¼ cup frozen chives
1 tablespoon horseradish mustard
Juice of ½ lemon
1 teaspoon onion salt

Mix all ingredients together. Refrigerate to allow flavors to set. Serve with crackers.

SHRIMP DIP

2 cans of shrimp
2 8-ounce packages of
 cream cheese
¾ cup finely chopped
 onion
1 teaspoon horseradish
Dash of Tabasco

Mix shrimp and softened cream cheese. Add onion, horseradish, and Tabasco. Let sit in refrigerator for a couple of hours. Serve with crackers.

LOUISE'S SHRIMP DIP

1 can tomato soup
3 3-ounce packages cream
 cheese
¼ cup warm water
1 package unflavored
 gelatin
¾ cup chopped green
 onions
¾ cup finely chopped
 celery, optional
1 cup mayonnaise
2 small cans shrimp,
 drained and diced

Heat soup and add cream cheese. Blend well and allow to cool. Dissolve gelatin in water and add to cooled soup. Add all other ingredients and chill. Serve with crackers.

Louise McCall

TANGY SHRIMP DIP

2	4½-ounce cans shrimp, rinsed and drained
1	3-ounce package cream cheese
⅓	cup Thousand Island dressing
¼	cup mayonnaise
⅓	cup salsa
2	tablespoons grated onion
1	teaspoon horseradish

Finely chop shrimp. Combine shrimp with remaining ingredients and mix well. Cover and refrigerate until chilled. Serve with crackers.

SPINACH DIP

1	10-ounce package frozen chopped spinach
1	package Knorr's vegetable soup mix
½	cup green onion, chopped
1	cup mayonnaise
1	cup sour cream

Thaw spinach and drain well. Add other ingredients and mix thoroughly. Refrigerate before serving. Serve with crackers.

For a change of taste add 2 cups of grated Swiss cheese.

QUICK SPINACH DIP

1	10-ounce package frozen chopped spinach
1	cup sour cream
1	tablespoon mayonnaise
1	tablespoon dry minced onion
1	small package dry ranch style buttermilk dressing

Thaw and drain the spinach. Mix all ingredients together and chill for several hours. Serve with corn chips.

EGG NOG

6   eggs, separated
1   pint whipping cream
1   pint half-and-half
¾   cup sugar

Whip egg whites until stiff. Add ¼ cup sugar to egg whites. Beat egg yolks and ½ cup sugar until well blended. Whip cream until stiff. Blend all ingredients and fold until well mixed. Refrigerate. Add nutmeg and spirits (if desired) just before serving.

Makes about 6 cups

HOT CHOCOLATE MIX

8   quarts powdered milk
1   1-pound carton dry Nestle's Quik
6   ounces powdered non-dairy creamer
½   cup powdered sugar

Mix all ingredients and store in a large tightly sealed container. To serve, fill a coffee mug half way with mix and add boiling water.

Marti Clinesmith

SPICE TEA MIX

2   cups Tang
1   cup sugar
½   cup instant tea
1   teaspoon grated lemon peel
1   teaspoon grated orange peel
1   teaspoon cinnamon
½   teaspoon grated cloves

Mix all ingredients and store in a tightly sealed container or glass jar. Use 2 teaspoons per cup with boiling water.

Mom

IRISH CREAM

1¼ cups Irish whiskey
1 14-ounce can sweetened condensed milk
1 cup whipping cream
4 eggs
2 tablespoons chocolate syrup
2 teaspoons instant coffee
1 teaspoon almond extract
1 teaspoon vanilla extract

Mix all ingredients in blender. Refrigerate. Serve cold.

Will keep in the refrigerator for two weeks.

Makes twelve 2-ounce servings

WARM HOLIDAY PUNCH

2 1-quart bottles cranberry juice
1 12-ounce can frozen apple juice concentrate
3½ cups water
6 cinnamon sticks
6 whole cloves
1 teaspoon allspice

Combine all ingredients in a large pot. Heat.

Serves 8

CRANBERRY PUNCH

1 quart cranberry juice
1 46-ounce can pineapple juice
1½ cups sugar
1 teaspoon almond extract
1 quart ginger ale

Combine first four ingredients. Chill. Just before serving, add ginger ale. Serve over ice.

Makes thirty two (32) 4-ounce servings

Soups and Salads

BAKED POTATO SOUP

6   slices bacon, fried crisp, save drippings
1   cup onion, chopped
⅔   cup flour
6   cups chicken broth
4   cups potatoes, baked, peeled and diced
2   cups heavy cream
¼   cup chopped parsley
1½   teaspoons garlic, granulated
1½   teaspoons basil
1½   teaspoons salt
1½   teaspoons red pepper sauce
1½   teaspoons black pepper
1   cup grated Cheddar cheese
¼   cup green onion, chopped

Crumble bacon. Cook onions in bacon drippings until transparent. Add flour, stirring constantly for 3 to 5 minutes or until mixture begins to turn golden. Gradually add chicken broth, stirring constantly until liquid thickens. Reduce heat to simmer and add potatoes, cream, crumbled bacon, parsley, garlic, basil, salt, pepper sauce and pepper. Simmer for 10 minutes. Do not let boil. Add grated cheese and green onions. Heat until cheese melts. Just before serving, top with additional bacon and cheese.

Makes 2 quarts and serves 8

BROCCOLI CHEESE SOUP

6   tablespoons butter or margarine
¼   cup onion, chopped
½   cup flour
1   can chicken broth
1   cup milk
1   10-ounce package frozen chopped broccoli, cooked until tender
1   pound Velveeta cheese, grated

Sauté onion in 2 tablespoons butter. In a large saucepan melt 4 tablespoons butter and add flour. Stir until well blended. Slowly add milk and stir constantly over low heat until mixture begins to thicken. Add chicken broth and keep stirring until smooth and creamy. Add broccoli onions, and then cheese. Heat until cheese is completely melted.

Serves 4 to 6

CORN CHOWDER

6 slices bacon
1 medium onion, chopped
2 medium potatoes, peeled and cubed
½ cup water
2 cups milk
1 17-ounce can cream style corn
1 teaspoon salt
Dash of pepper

Fry bacon in a Dutch oven until crisp. Remove bacon reserving 2 tablespoons of bacon drippings in pan. Crumble bacon and set aside. Sauté onion in reserved drippings until tender. Add potatoes and water. Cover and simmer 15 to 20 minutes or until potatoes are tender. Stir in milk, corn, salt and pepper. Cook over medium heat, stirring frequently until thoroughly heated. Sprinkle with bacon before serving.

Makes 5 cups

MEXICAN SOUP

1½ pounds ground meat
1 onion, chopped
2 cans stewed tomatoes
2 cans Ranch style beans
2 cans corn
2 packages dry Ranch style dressing
1½ packages taco seasoning
1 can chopped green chilies

Brown meat and onions. Drain thoroughly. Add dry seasonings followed by all other ingredients. Cook over low heat 45 minutes.

Serves 8

TORTILLA SOUP

1 tablespoon oil
2 cloves garlic, minced
1 medium onion, chopped
2 cans whole peeled tomatoes
¼ cup diced Rotel tomatoes
8 cups chicken broth
1 teaspoon ground cumin
1 teaspoon white pepper
4 chicken breasts, boiled and diced
Corn tortillas
1 avocado, diced
8 ounces Monterey Jack cheese

Sauté garlic and onion in oil. Puree tomatoes and Rotel. Combine with garlic and onions in large sauce pan and cook over low heat for about 15 minutes. Add chicken broth, cumin and pepper. Continue simmering for another 30 minutes. Cut corn tortillas in strips and fry in a small amount of oil until crisp. Drain well. When ready to serve, partially fill bowls with broth and add chicken, avocado, cheese and tortilla strips.

Serves 8

SHRIMP BISQUE

1 pound shrimp, cooked and peeled
4 tablespoons butter
4-5 tablespoons flour
1 quart milk
2 teaspoons salt
3 teaspoons lemon juice
½ teaspoon Tabasco
Sherry

Finely mince shrimp in blender or food processor. Melt butter in a large saucepan and stir in flour. Add milk and salt; stir until thickened. Add lemon juice and Tabasco. Add shrimp and heat thoroughly. When serving, add sherry, if desired, to each bowl (one to two tablespoons per serving).

Serves 6

SHRIMP GUMBO

2 pounds raw shrimp
4 tablespoons oil, divided use
2 tablespoons flour
2 onions, chopped
3 cups okra, chopped
3 garlic cloves, minced
1 can whole tomatoes, chopped
2 quarts water
1 bay leaf
1 teaspoon salt
Tabasco

Peel and devein shrimp. Make a dark roux of 2 tablespoons oil and flour. Set aside. Sauté onions, okra and garlic in 2 tablespoons oil. Add tomatoes and juice when okra is nearly done. Add sautéed vegetables, roux, shrimp and all other ingredients. Cook slowly for 30 minutes.

Serves 8

Louise McCall

STEAK SOUP

1 stick butter
½ cup flour
4 cans beef consommé
¾ cup diced carrots
¾ cup diced celery, optional
¾ cup diced onions
1 14.5-ounce can tomatoes, diced
¾ cup barley
1 small can corn
2 medium potatoes, diced
2 beef bouillon cubes
1 tablespoon black pepper
1 clove garlic, minced
1 tablespoon Accent
1 tablespoon oil
1½ tablespoons Kitchen Bouquet
2 pounds round steak, cut in ¼-inch cubes

Melt butter in a heavy soup pot. Add flour and stir to form a smooth paste, stirring constantly. Cook over medium heat without browning, for 3 minutes. Again, stir constantly. Add consommé and stir until smooth and slightly thickened. Bring to a full boil and add all other ingredients except oil, Kitchen Bouquet and meat. Allow to reach a full boil then reduce heat and simmer for 30 minutes. Stir frequently. In a skillet, brown the meat in oil and Kitchen Bouquet. Add to soup and simmer for 3½ hours.

Freezes well.

Serves 10 to 12

THREE DAY VEGGIE SOUP

DAY 1

2	pounds stew meat
1	large onion, chopped
1	large soup bone
8-10	cups water
2	bay leaves
2	stalks celery, optional

Place all in a large soup pot and bring to a boil. Turn down heat and simmer 2 to 3 hours. Refrigerate.

DAY 2

6	potatoes, peeled and chopped
6	carrots, peeled and chopped
2	large cans stewed tomatoes
1	8-ounce can tomato paste
	Salt and pepper to taste

Skim off fat from top of pot. Remove and discard soup bone. Remove meat, trim and cut into bite size pieces. Heat broth, add meat and remaining ingredients. Simmer 2 to 3 hours. Refrigerate.

DAY 3

1	large can whole kernel corn
	Additional vegetables, as desired

Add corn and any desired vegetables. Heat until hot and serve with cornbread.

Freezes well.

Serves 8 to 10

Marti Clinesmith

INSTANT VICHYSSOISE

2	10-ounce cans condensed chicken broth
1	3¼-ounce individual package Pillsbury "Idaho Mashed Potatoes" Granules - No substitute
1	teaspoon celery salt
1	teaspoon onion powder
2	cups half-and-half

Place broth in saucepan. Add seasonings and bring to a boil. Add potato granules and stir out lumps. Blend in half-and-half and cool. Refrigerate and serve very cold.

Serves 4 to 6

Sue Geren

Apricot-Pineapple Salad

1   large can apricots, drain and save juice
1   large can crushed pineapple, drain and save juice
2   packages orange Jell-O
2   cups boiling water
2   cups combined apricot and pineapple juice
½   cup sugar
3   tablespoons flour
1   egg, slightly beaten
2   tablespoons butter
1   cup heavy cream, whipped
¾   cup grated cheese, optional

Dice apricots, combine with pineapple and chill. Dissolve Jell-O in boiling water. Add 1 cup reserved juice. Chill until slightly congealed. Fold in fruit. Pour into 9x11-inch shallow pan. Chill until firm. For topping, combine sugar and flour, blend in egg and other cup of reserved juice. Stir over low heat until thickened. Remove from heat, stir in butter and cool completely. Fold in whipped cream and spread over gelatin mixture. Sprinkle with grated cheese. Chill and cut into squares.

Serves 10 to 12

Quick Cranberry Salad

1   small can crushed pineapple
1   3-ounce package strawberry Jell-O
1   cup boiling water
1   16-ounce can jellied cranberry sauce
½   cup cold liquid (reserved pineapple juice and water to make ½ cup)
2   teaspoons lemon juice

Drain pineapple, reserving juices. Dissolve Jell-O in hot water. While still warm, stir in cranberry sauce and mix until melted. Stir in ½ cup cold liquid, lemon juice and pineapple. Pour into 1½-quart mold and chill until set.

FRUIT SALAD DRESSING

2   tablespoons mayonnaise
2   tablespoons sour cream
½   teaspoon sugar

Blend all dressing ingredients together. Spoon on Jell-O when serving.

Serves 6 to 8

COCONUT BANANAS

4   ripe bananas
4   tablespoons lemon
     juice
1   16-ounce carton sour
     cream
1¾ cups shredded coconut

Peel and cut bananas diagonally into 1-inch segments. Place lemon juice, sour cream, and coconut in separate bowls. Dip bananas into lemon juice, roll in sour cream, and then in coconut. Be sure to cover thoroughly. Place on a platter or cookie sheet and refrigerate for several hours or overnight.

Serves 6 to 8

FRUIT SALAD

1   small box vanilla
     pudding, not instant
1   box tapioca
1   large can mandarin
     oranges
1   medium can pineapple
     tidbits or chunks
3   bananas
1   cup juice from
     mandarin oranges
1   cup juice from
     pineapples
½   cup orange juice
Maraschino cherries

Cook pudding and tapioca in the fruit juices until thickened. If either can does not provide 1 cup of liquid, simply add enough orange juice to make 2½ cups of liquid. Let cool. Add fruit. Pour into a round serving dish and chill.

Serves 6 to 8

Jean Daume

AVOCADO-TOMATO SALAD

1   large tomato
1   avocado, ripe not mushy
3   green onions, chopped
Garlic salt to taste
Pepper to taste
½   cup poppy seed dressing

Dice tomato and avocado. Add green onions and season to taste. Gently stir in poppy seed dressing.

Serves 4

Vers

STRAWBERRY SALAD

2   packages strawberry Jell-O
1   cup boiling water
2   10-ounce packages frozen strawberries, thawed and undrained
1   1-pound 4-ounce can crushed pineapple, drained
2   8-ounce cartons sour cream

Dissolve Jell-O in water. Add strawberries with juice, and drained pineapple. Put half of Jell-O in a 3-quart rectangular Pyrex dish which has been greased with mayonnaise or vegetable spray and refrigerate until firm. When congealed, spread sour cream over top. Pour remaining Jell-O over sour cream and refrigerate.

Serves 10 to 12

RASPBERRY SALAD

2   cans frozen red raspberries
1   20-ounce can crushed pineapple
1   small can frozen orange juice, thawed and undiluted
1   cup boiling water
2   packages red raspberry Jell-O

Thaw and drain raspberries. Drain pineapple. Reserve juices. Add thawed orange juice to drained juice to make 2½ cups. Dissolve Jell-O in boiling water. Add juices and chill until partially set. Add the raspberries and pineapple. Put the mixture in a 1½ to 2-quart mold and chill until set.

Serves 10 to 12

BLUEBERRY JELL-O SALAD

1   box lemon Jell-O
1   box raspberry Jell-O
1   tablespoon lemon juice
1   cup boiling water
½   cup cold water
1   can blueberry pie filling
1   cup sour cream
¼   cup powdered sugar

Mix gelatins with boiling water until dissolved. Add cold water and lemon juice. Add pie filling. Pour into 9x13-inch dish and refrigerate until firm. Mix sour cream and powdered sugar and spread on top of gelatin.

Serves 12

Mom

41

ARTICHOKE AND RICE SALAD

1   6-ounce package of chicken flavor Rice-a-Roni
1   6-ounce jar marinated artichoke hearts, reserve liquid
⅓   cup Hellmann's mayonnaise
4   green onions and tops, chopped
1   small can sliced ripe olives
Dash of Tabasco

Cook Rice-a-Roni according to package directions. Coarsely chop artichoke hearts and add to prepared rice. Mix mayonnaise, curry powder, green onions, olives and artichoke liquid. Add to rice mixture. Gently mix all ingredients well and refrigerate until served.

For a hearty salad, add two coarsely chopped, cooked chicken breasts.

May add ½ cup chopped bell pepper and/or 1 can water chestnuts, chopped. May substitute sliced, stuffed green olives for ripe olives.

Serves 6 to 8

Sue Geren

BLACK-EYED PEA SALAD

3   15-ounce cans black-eyed peas, drained
1   cup chopped onion
1   cup chopped green onion
1½ cups chopped red bell pepper
½   cup chopped and seed jalapeños
½   teaspoon minced garlic
2   cups Italian dressing

Mix all of the above and refrigerate.

Serves 6 to 8

Chicken and Rice Salad

3 cups cooked rice
1½ cups cooked chicken (white meat), diced
½ toasted slivered almonds
⅓ cup minced green onion
¼ cup chopped parsley

Combine all salad ingredients and mix well.

SPICY DRESSING

¾ cup mayonnaise
2 tablespoons soy sauce
1½ tablespoons curry powder
1 tablespoon vinegar
¼ teaspoon garlic powder

Combine all dressing ingredients in a saucepan and heat thoroughly. Add dressing to salad, toss and chill thoroughly.

Serves 5

California Coleslaw

2 tablespoons sesame seeds
½ cup slivered almonds, toasted
1 medium head of lettuce, chopped
4 green onions, chopped
1 package chicken flavored Ramen noodle soup mix

Crush noodles by hand and mix all salad ingredients together. Do not use the soup seasoning packet.

VINAIGRETTE DRESSING

2 tablespoons sugar
½ cup salad oil
3 tablespoons raspberry vinegar
½ teaspoon salt
½ teaspoon pepper

Combine all dressing ingredients and shake until well mixed. Add the dressing to the lettuce mixture and toss. This will keep in the refrigerator for up to 5 days.

Serves 6 to 8

Jan Sloan Sly

CHINESE COLESLAW

1   package coleslaw mix
1   package Ramen soup
    mix, any flavor
2   green onions, chopped
1   small package slivered
    almonds, toasted
2   tablespoons sugar
3   tablespoons sesame
    seeds, toasted
¾   cup oil

Mix coleslaw, onions, broken Ramen noodles, toasted almonds and sesame seeds. In a separate bowl, combine oil, sugar and soup flavoring packet. Pour dressing on salad and toss. If not served immediately, do not add dressing until serving.

Serves 6

CURRIED COLESLAW

1   small cabbage,
    shredded (about 3 to 4
    cups)
¼   cup raisins
2   tablespoons minced
    onion
½   cup mayonnaise
1   tablespoon raspberry
    vinegar
1   teaspoon sugar
½   teaspoon curry powder
4   slices bacon, cooked
    and crumbled

Combine cabbage, raisins and onion. In a separate bowl, mix mayonnaise, vinegar, sugar, and curry powder. Pour over cabbage mixture and toss. Cover and chill. Add bacon just before serving.

Serves 4 to 6

JILL'S BERMUDA JALAPEÑO MACARONI SALAD

1	12-ounce package small seashell macaroni
1	teaspoon garlic salt
1	teaspoon celery salt
1	teaspoon onion salt
2	teaspoons celery seeds
2	cups mayonnaise
1	medium lemon, juiced
1	small can jalapeños, chopped; drain and reserve liquid
1	large onion, chopped
1	medium bell pepper
½	cup finely chopped celery, optional
¼	cup chopped pimentos

Cook macaroni in boiling water until tender. Rinse with hot water. While macaroni is still warm, add garlic salt, celery salt, onion salt and celery seeds. Let sit for 15 minutes. In a separate bowl, mix mayonnaise and lemon juice. Add half of the mayonnaise mixture to the macaroni. Stir in jalapeño, onion, green pepper, pimento and celery. Add the remainder of the mayonnaise mixture. Refrigerate for several hours before serving.

Add jalapeño juice for an even spicier taste.

Serves 8 to 10

Linda Wood

SAUERKRAUT SALAD

1	20-ounce jar sauerkraut
¾	cup celery, finely chopped
¾	cup onion, finely chopped
¾	cup green onion, finely chopped
½	cup vinegar
½	cup salad oil
1	cup sugar

Mix vinegar, salad oil and sugar. Add all other ingredients and marinate for several days.

Great as a salad or on sandwiches.

Marion Culbertson

BLACK BEAN POTATO SALAD

3 pounds small red new potatoes
4 scallions, thinly sliced
5 radishes, chopped
1 15-ounce can black beans, drained and rinsed
¼ cup non-fat plain yogurt
¼ cup low-fat salad dressing
3 tablespoons Dijon mustard
1 tablespoon white balsamic vinegar
1 tablespoon fresh cracked pepper
1 tablespoon fresh dill, chopped

Scrub potatoes and cut into large bite-sized pieces. Boil until slightly soft, 10 to 15 minutes. Drain and cool. In a large bowl, combine potatoes, scallions, radishes and beans. In a small bowl whisk together yogurt, salad dressing, mustard, vinegar, pepper and dill. Pour dressing over salad and lightly toss.

Other fresh herbs may be substituted for dill.

Serves 4 to 6

Mark Doton

FRENCH POTATO SALAD

6 medium new potatoes
3 tablespoons chopped scallions
1 tablespoons chopped chives
3 tablespoons chopped red bell peppers
2 tablespoons chopped black olives
1 6.5-ounce package garlic & herb cheese spread
6 tablespoons olive oil
2 tablespoons balsamic vinegar
1 teaspoon minced shallots

Steam and cube potatoes and allow to cool. Combine potatoes, scallions, chives, red peppers and olives in a bowl. In a separate bowl, whisk together olive oil, vinegar and shallots until well blended. In a medium mixing bowl, whisk cheese spread and gradually add oil and vinegar mixture. If the sauce appears to be too thick, simply add a little milk. Toss potatoes with about ½ cup of sauce. Refrigerate until ready to serve.

Use remaining sauce as a dip.

Serves 4

REGATTA SALAD

1   pound cooked chicken
    breasts, diced
¾   cup cooked corn
½   cup sliced mushrooms
2   cups cooked white rice
2   shallots, chopped
2   tablespoons chopped
    parsley
2   peaches, diced
1   ripe avocado, diced
1   lemon, juiced

REGATTA DRESSING

¾   cup mayonnaise
2   ounces whipping
    cream, whipped
2   tablespoons lemon
    juice
2   teaspoons curry powder
1   teaspoon salt
½   teaspoon black pepper
½   teaspoon cayenne
    pepper

Drizzle lemon juice over
peaches and avocados.
Refrigerate. In a large bowl,
mix chicken, corn, mushrooms,
rice, shallots and parsley. Add
dressing and chill. Add peaches
and avocados when ready to
serve.

Mix all dressing ingredients.

Serves 6

Kathy Daume

ALOHA SHRIMP SALAD

2   pounds cooked shrimp
1   cup finely chopped
    celery, optional
1   20-ounce can
    unsweetened pineapple
    chunks, drained
⅓   cup raisins
½   cup reduced calorie
    mayonnaise
2   teaspoons curry powder

Combine all ingredients, cover
and chill at least 1 hour. Serve
on leaf lettuce.

Serves 6 to 8

Mary White

SPAGHETTI SALAD

1	red onion, chopped
1½	tomatoes, diced
1½	cucumbers, diced
8	ounces thin spaghetti
1	8-ounce bottle Italian dressing
4	tablespoons McCormick's Salad Supreme spice

Cook spaghetti until tender. Drain and cool completely. Add all other ingredients and mix well. Refrigerate for several hours before serving.

Serves 6 to 8

SPINACH CHICKEN SALAD

1	bunch or bag of fresh spinach, rinsed and broken into bite size pieces
1	cup cooked, diced white meat chicken
1	large can mandarin oranges, drained
1	large avocado, diced
1	can fried onion rings

Garlic salt to taste
Pepper to taste

Mix all and serve with Honey Mustard Dressing (see index)

Serves 6 to 8

Kathy Daume

SPRING SALAD

½ pound fresh asparagus
1 6-ounce jar marinated artichoke hearts, liquid reserved
½ cup sliced fresh mushrooms
¼ cup sliced green onion
1 tablespoon vinegar
1 teaspoon sugar
1 teaspoon sesame seeds, toasted
¼ teaspoon salt
Dash of Tabasco sauce

Cook asparagus for 10 to 15 minutes. Drain. Place in a shallow dish. Slice artichokes in half and place over asparagus. Add mushrooms and onion. Combine reserved marinade, vinegar, sugar, sesame seeds, salt and pepper. Pour over vegetables and refrigerate several hours.

Serves 4

COLD VEGETABLE SALAD

1 package frozen broccoli florets or equivalent fresh
1 package frozen French style green beans
1 green pepper, seeded and chopped
1 cucumber, peeled and chopped
2 cans artichoke hearts, drained and quartered
1 can asparagus spears, drained and cut in half

Cook broccoli and green beans half the recommended time. Drain and chill. Layer in order: broccoli, green beans, green pepper, cucumber, artichoke and asparagus.

VEGETABLE SALAD DRESSING

1 cup mayonnaise
½ cup half-and-half
3 tablespoons lemon juice
3 tablespoons vinegar
½ teaspoon garlic powder
¼ cup chopped green onion

Combine and thoroughly mix all dressing ingredients. Pour on salad and marinate for 24 hours.

Serves 10 to 12

49

Tomato Aspic

1½ packages unflavored
    gelatin
¾ cup water
1 can tomato soup
⅓ soup can water
½ teaspoon garlic powder
½ teaspoon celery salt
½ teaspoon onion salt
¼ teaspoon powdered
    cloves
1 tablespoon
    Worcestershire
1 tablespoon lemon juice

Dissolve gelatin in ¾ cup water. Combine soup, additional water, garlic powder, celery salt, onion salt and cloves. Bring to boil and add gelatin, Worcestershire sauce and lemon juice. Bring back to a boil and cook for several minutes. Pour into individual custard cups and chill until set.

Serves 8

Esther Stonestreet

Marinated Vegetable Salad

1 14-ounce can artichoke
    hearts, drained and
    sliced in half
1 16-ounce can whole
    green beans, drained
1 small can pitted ripe
    black olives, drained
½ pound fresh
    mushrooms
1 medium purple onion,
    sliced thin
Pepper to taste
1 cup sugar
1 cup vinegar
1 teaspoon salt
3 tablespoons Italian
    dressing

In a bowl, combine artichoke hearts, green beans, olives and mushrooms. In a saucepan, combine sugar, vinegar, salt, Italian dressing and pepper to taste. Bring to a boil, stirring to dissolve sugar. Cool slightly and pour over vegetables. Refrigerate for at least 24 hours, stirring occasionally to be sure all ingredients are marinated.

Serves 4

JEZEBEL SAUCE

1 jar apple jelly
1 jar orange marmalade
1 jar apricot jam
1 jar fresh horseradish
½ small can Coleman's mustard

Combine all ingredients and put in jars. Refrigerate.

Keeps indefinitely.

Great with pork.

HONEY MUSTARD DRESSING

⅓ cup honey
¼ cup Dijon style mustard
1 clove garlic, minced
2 tablespoons fresh lemon juice
¼ cup rice wine vinegar
1 cup canola oil (or light vegetable oil)
½ teaspoon sesame oil

In a blender or food processor mix honey, mustard, garlic, lemon juice and vinegar. With motor running add canola oil and sesame oil in a slow stream. Process until smooth and creamy. Store in refrigerator.

Makes 1½ cups

Kathy Daume

HOT MUSTARD

1 4-ounce can Coleman's mustard
4 ounces flour
¾ cup sugar
1 teaspoon salt
White wine vinegar

Mix dry ingredients with enough wine vinegar to form desired consistency. Let sit in refrigerator for at least 24 hours before using.

If mustard becomes too thick, add more wine vinegar.

Vers

51

Poppy Seed Dressing

1½ cups sugar
2   teaspoons mild dry
    mustard
2   teaspoons salt
⅔   cup vinegar
3   tablespoons onion juice
    or 1 teaspoon onion
    powder
2   cups salad oil
3   tablespoons poppy
    seeds

Combine all ingredients and
mix until well blended.

Makes 3½ cups

Mom

Rémoulade Sauce

4   tablespoons olive oil or
    salad oil
2   tablespoons tarragon
    vinegar
1   teaspoon salt
2   tablespoons Creole
    mustard
½   teaspoon paprika
4   small green onions,
    minced
4   sprigs parsley, minced
10 tablespoons
    mayonnaise

Combine all ingredients and
chill for 12 to 24 hours.

Kathryn Zack

Brunch and Breads

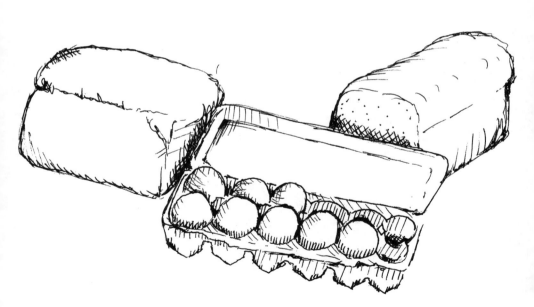

APPLE BREAKFAST LASAGNA

1 cup sour cream
⅓ cup brown sugar
2 6-piece packages frozen French toast
¾ pound thinly sliced ham
3 cups Sargento 3 Cheese Gourmet Recipe Blend
1 21-ounce can apple pie filling
1 cup granola with raisins
¼ cup pecans, chopped, optional

Preheat oven to 350°. In a small bowl, blend sour cream and brown sugar, chill. Place 6 French toast slices in bottom of greased 13x9-inch baking pan. Layer ham, 1½ cups cheese and remaining 6 slices of French toast. Spread apple pie filling over top, sprinkle with granola and nuts, if desired. Bake for 25 minutes, then top with remaining 1½ cups cheese and bake for 5 additional minutes. Serve with chilled sour cream and brown sugar mixture.

Serves 6

Anne DeuPree Duke

BRUNCH CASSEROLE

6 hard-boiled eggs, sliced
Salt and pepper
1 pound hot bulk sausage, cooked and drained
1½ cups sour cream
½ cup dry bread crumbs
1½ cups Cheddar cheese, grated

Line bottom of a greased casserole with eggs. Season to taste. Sprinkle sausage over eggs. Gently spread sour cream over sausage. Combine bread crumbs and cheese and sprinkle on top of casserole. Bake at 350° for 20 minutes or until heated through. Brown top under broiler watching carefully. May be prepared the night before and refrigerated until baking. Increase baking time as needed if casserole is refrigerated ahead of baking.

Serves 6

BACON & EGG CASSEROLE

1	dozen hard-boiled eggs, sliced
1½	pounds bacon, cooked crisp and crumbled
9	tablespoons butter
9	tablespoons flour
3	cups milk
½	pound jar Cheese Whiz or ½-pound Velveeta
¼	teaspoon thyme
¼	teaspoon basil
¼	teaspoon marjoram
¼	cup parsley flakes
2	tablespoons minced onion

Make a medium cream sauce by melting the butter in a large saucepan. Stir in the flour until blended. Slowly add the milk, stirring constantly until sauce has thickened. Add cheese and seasonings to cream sauce. If the sauce is too thick, simply add a little more milk. Layer half of sauce on the bottom of a 9x13-inch greased casserole. Add eggs then bacon and top with the other half of the sauce. Sprinkle cracker crumbs on top of sauce. Bake at 350° for about 30 minutes or until bubbly and lightly browned.

May be made the day before baking. Refrigerate until ready to bake.

Serves 8 to 10

Mom

COMPANY EGGS

½	pound Gruyère cheese, grated
4	tablespoons butter
1	cup heavy cream
½	teaspoon salt
Pepper	
1½	teaspoons dry mustard
12	eggs, slightly beaten

Grease a 9x13-inch casserole. Spread cheese in bottom of baking dish. Dot with butter. Mix cream with seasonings and mustard. Pour half of liquid over cheese. Add eggs and then remaining half of cream mixture. Bake at 325° for about 35 minutes or until eggs are set.

Serves 8 to 10

CHARLOTTE'S SAUSAGE CASSEROLE

1	pound hot Jimmy Dean sausage
1	pound regular Jimmy Dean sausage
2½	cups Brownberry onion/garlic croutons
4	eggs
2½	cups milk
¾	teaspoons dry mustard
2	cups grated sharp Old English cheese
2	cups grated Velveeta
1	can cream of mushroom soup
½	cup milk

Brown and drain sausage. Place in greased 9x13-inch casserole. Top with croutons. Mix eggs, milk, mustard and pour over croutons. Add cheese next. Cover with foil. Refrigerate 12 hours. Just before baking, combine soup and milk and pour over casserole. Bake at 350° uncovered for 45 minutes.

Serves 10

Sharon Neves

BREAKFAST PIZZA

1	pound pork sausage
1	8-ounce package refrigerated crescent rolls
1	cup frozen hash brown potatoes, thawed
1	cup shredded Cheddar cheese
5	eggs
½	cup milk
½	teaspoon salt
⅛	teaspoon pepper
2	tablespoons freshly grated Parmesan cheese

Brown sausage and drain. Separate crescent dough into 8 triangles. Place on an ungreased 12-inch pizza pan with points toward the center. Press over bottom and up sides to form a pizza crust. Sprinkle with potatoes. Spoon sausage over crust and top with Cheddar cheese. In a bowl, beat together eggs, milk, salt, and pepper. Pour into crust. Top with Parmesan cheese. Bake at 375° for 25 to 30 minutes.

Serves 6 to 8

EGG AND ARTICHOKE CASSEROLE

1	bunch green onions
1	clove garlic
2	6-ounce jars marinated artichoke hearts
6	eggs
12	ounces sharp Cheddar cheese, grated
½	cup cracker crumbs
½	teaspoon pepper

Trim onions at the base and halfway up the green tops. Mince finely with peeled garlic clove. Remove artichokes from jars, reserving marinade. Cut artichokes into thirds and set aside. Sauté onions and garlic in marinade. Beat eggs in small mixing bowl. Add artichoke hearts, sautéed onions and garlic, pepper and grated Cheddar cheese. Stir in cracker crumbs and pour mixture into a greased 9-inch square baking dish or pan. Bake until firm and golden brown. Do not overcook. Cut into squares at once and serve.

Refrigerate or freeze leftovers and reheat 15 to 20 minutes in a 350° oven or 2 to 3 minutes in the microwave.

This dish does not have to be kept hot while serving. It keeps its shape and taste at room temperature. It can be prepared a day ahead and refrigerated or frozen.

Serves 4

Anne DeuPree Duke

GREEN CHILI AND CHEESE SOUFFLÉ

2   cups grated Monterey
    Jack cheese
2   cups grated Cheddar
    cheese
1   4.5-ounce can chopped
    green chilies
4   eggs, separated
⅔   cup evaporated milk
1   tablespoon flour
½   teaspoon salt
⅛   teaspoon pepper
2   tomatoes, sliced

Grease soufflé dish. Combine cheeses and green chilies in bottom of dish. Beat egg whites until stiff. Mix egg yolk with milk, flour, and seasonings. Fold into egg whites. Pour into dish over cheeses and chilies. Bake at 350° for 30 minutes. Top with sliced tomatoes and bake an additional 30 minutes.

Serves 6 to 8

HAM & EGG CASSEROLE

3   cups frozen shredded
    hash brown potatoes
¾   cup grated Monterey
    Jack cheese
1   cup diced ham or
    Canadian bacon
¼   cup chopped green
    onion
4   eggs, beaten
1   12-ounce can
    evaporated milk
¼   teaspoon pepper
⅛   teaspoon salt

Coat a 2-quart square baking dish with cooking spray. Place potatoes evenly on the bottom of the dish. Sprinkle with cheese, ham and green onion. In a mixing bowl combine eggs, milk, salt, and pepper. Pour this mixture over the potatoes. Cover and refrigerate several hours or overnight. Bake uncovered at 350° for approximately 1 hour.

Serves 6

HEARTY BRUNCH CASSEROLE

½ pound bacon, sliced into small pieces
1 medium onion, chopped
1 32-ounce bag frozen hash brown potatoes
12 eggs
2 4.5-ounce cans chopped green chilies
1 pound grated Cheddar cheese
1 8-ounce jar salsa

Brown bacon. Add onions and sauté. Remove bacon and onions. Add hash browns and cook until lightly browned. Return bacon and onions to potatoes. In a separate dish, beat eggs until frothy. Add chilies to eggs. Spray a 9x13-inch casserole with cooking spray and layer hash brown mixture. Pour egg and chili mixture over potatoes. Cover casserole with cheese. Bake at 350° for 45 minutes or until eggs are set. Serve with salsa.

Serves 8

MAÑANA CASSEROLE

6 English muffins
6 tablespoons softened butter
1 pound pork sausage
3 cups grated Cheddar cheese
1 4.5-ounce can chopped green chilies
12 eggs, beaten
1½ cups sour cream

Grease a 13x9x2-inch casserole. Split and butter the English muffins and place buttered side down in the casserole. Brown and drain the sausage. Layer the sausage, cheese and green chilies on top of the muffins. Combine eggs and sour cream and pour over the casserole. Cover and refrigerate at least 8 hours. Remove and let stand 30 minutes before baking uncovered at 350° for 35 to 40 minutes.

Serves 8

OVERNIGHT EGG CASSEROLE

1   dozen large eggs,
     beaten
½   milk or cream
Salt and pepper to taste
1   teaspoon butter
1   8-ounce carton sour
     cream
12   slices bacon, cooked
     crisp, drained and
     crumbled
2   ounces grated Cheddar
     cheese
2   ounces grated Jack
     cheese

Melt butter in large skillet. Combine eggs, milk, salt and pepper and pour into skillet. Cook until barely set. Cool and stir in sour cream. Place egg mixture into a well buttered 2-quart rectangular baking dish. Top with cheese and bacon. Cover and refrigerate overnight. Bake uncovered at 350° for 30 minutes.

Serves 6 to 8

PAM'S BREAKFAST SOUFFLÉ

8   slices day-old bread,
     crusts removed
4   tablespoons butter,
     softened
½   pound Old English
     cheese, grated
6   eggs
3   cups milk
¼   teaspoon dry mustard
¼   teaspoon salt
¼   teaspoon pepper

Coat a 2-quart casserole with cooking spray. Butter both sides of the bread and cut each slice into ½-inch squares. In a separate mixing bowl, combine eggs, milk, mustard, salt and pepper. Blend well. In the greased casserole, layer half of the bread followed by half of the cheese. Repeat the layers. Pour the egg mixture over the bread and cheese. Refrigerate overnight. Bake at 350° for 45 minutes to 1 hour. Serve immediately.

Serves 6 to 8

Pam Mahoney

SAUSAGE CASSEROLE

1½ pounds sausage
1 8-ounce package refrigerated crescent dinner rolls
2 cups shredded Mozzarella cheese
4 eggs, beaten
¾ cup milk
Salt and pepper

Crumble and brown sausage. Drain well. Line bottom of greased 9x13-inch baking dish with rolls. Press perforations together to seal. Sprinkle sausage and cheese over dough. Combine liquid ingredients and pour over casserole. Bake at 425° for 15 minutes. Let stand 5 to 10 minutes before serving.

Serves 8

Marti Clinesmith

SAUSAGE ROLLS

2 loaves frozen bread dough
1 pound hot sausage
1 medium onion, chopped
1 medium green pepper, chopped
1 small can chopped green chilies
1 clove garlic, chopped
1 cup grated Cheddar cheese
1 cup grated Monterey Jack cheese

Thaw bread dough overnight in refrigerator. Sauté onion, green pepper, chilies and garlic. Brown sausage in the same skillet as the vegetables. Drain grease. Flatten bread dough and put half of the meat mixture down the middle of each. Add cheese. Pinch dough together to seal. Place loaves on greased aluminum foil covered cookie sheet. Bake for 30 minutes at 350°.

Makes 2 loaves and serves 8 to 10

Kathy Daume

61

SAUSAGE SWIRLS

1   8-ounce package refrigerated crescent rolls
1   pound sage flavored sausage, uncooked

Open rolls and smooth out dough to form a rectangle making sure all perforation marks are gone. Cover completely with sausage. Roll carefully into a log. Wrap in wax paper and freeze until able to slice easily, not solid. Slice into ¼-inch swirls. Place on an ungreased cookie sheet and bake at 350° for 20 minutes or until sausage is cooked and dough is lightly browned.

Makes about 30 swirls

SWISS CHEESE AND EGG CASSEROLE

2   cups soft bread cubes, crusts removed
1¾ cups half-and-half
8   eggs, slightly beaten
2   tablespoons butter
1   teaspoon seasoned salt
½   teaspoon pepper
1   cup shredded Swiss cheese
8   slices bacon, cooked crisp and crumbled
½   cup dry, fine bread crumbs
2   tablespoons melted butter

Combine bread cubes with half-and-half in a bowl and let soak five minutes. Drain liquid from bread and add to beaten eggs. Mix well. Melt 2 tablespoons of butter in a skillet and add egg mixture. Softly scramble eggs. When eggs are still soft but almost cooked through, add soaked bread cubes. Stir to combine. Season with salt and pepper. Pour egg mixture into a lightly greased casserole. Top with cheese, bacon and dry bread crumbs. Drizzle top with melted butter. Bake at 400° for 10 to 15 minutes, or until heated through and cheese is melted.

Serves 8

SWISS CHEESE SOUFFLÉ

¼ cup butter or margarine
¼ cup flour
¼ teaspoon salt
1½ cups milk
1 teaspoon Dijon mustard
2 cups (½-pound) shredded or grated Swiss cheese
4 eggs, separated

Melt butter in a saucepan over low heat. Blend in the flour and salt. Stir in milk. Cook and stir over medium heat until mixture is smooth and thickened. Remove from heat and add mustard and cheese, stirring until cheese is melted. Beat in egg yolks, one at a time. Beat the egg whites until stiff and fold into cheese mixture. Pour into a greased 1½ to 2-quart soufflé or baking dish. Bake at 375° for 30 to 40 minutes or until firm and well browned. Serve immediately.

Serves 4 to 6

CHEESE GRITS SOUFFLÉ

1 cup grits
1 stick butter
3 cups sharp Cheddar cheese, grated
4 eggs, separated
¼ cup half-and-half
Dash of Worcestershire sauce
Salt and pepper to taste

Slightly beat egg yolks. Stiffly beat egg whites. Cook grits until thick and smooth according to directions on package. Stir in butter, 2 cups cheese, egg yolks, half-and-half, Worcestershire sauce and seasoning. Fold in egg whites and spoon into a greased 2-quart casserole. Bake at 350° for 30 minutes. Sprinkle with remaining cheese and bake 15 minutes longer.

Serves 8 to 10

GARLIC CHEESE GRITS

1   cup uncooked grits
½   cup butter
1   6-ounce roll garlic
    cheese
2   eggs
Milk
Dash of Tabasco
Dash of Worcestershire
    sauce

Cook grits according to package directions. Stir in butter and garlic cheese and continue cooking until cheese is melted. Break eggs into a measuring cup and add enough milk to make 1 cup. Beat this mixture well and then add to hot grits mixture. Add Tabasco and Worcestershire sauce. Bake in a greased 2-quart casserole at 350° for 1 hour.

Serves 6 to 8

SCALLOPED PINEAPPLE

4   cups fresh bread
    crumbs
1   20-ounce can pineapple
    chunks, drained
3   eggs, beaten
2   cups sugar
1   cup butter, melted

Toss together bread crumbs and pineapple and place in a greased 2-quart baking dish. Combine eggs, sugar and melted butter and pour over pineapple. Bake at 350° for 30 minutes.

Can be made up and refrigerated overnight before baking.

Reheats well. Serve with ham.

Serves 8

Sue Geren

HOT CURRIED FRUIT

1   package frozen mixed
    fruit, thawed
1   can pitted Bing cherries
2   bananas, sliced
½   cup brown sugar
1   tablespoon curry
    powder
1   tablespoon corn starch
¼   cup butter or margarine

Drain fruit. Combine dry ingredients and sprinkle over fruit and gently toss. Use butter to grease casserole - if there is any remaining, leave in bottom of dish. Add fruit to dish and bake at 350° for 40 minutes.

Serves 4

Marti Clinesmith

BELGIAN WAFFLES

4   eggs, separated
½   teaspoon vanilla
3   tablespoons butter or
    margarine, melted
1   cup flour
½   teaspoon salt
1   cup milk

Beat egg yolks until very light. Add vanilla and butter. Combine flour and salt; add with milk to egg mixture. Beat well. Beat egg whites until stiff and fold into batter. Bake in waffle iron until lightly browned.

Serves 4 to 6

WAFFLES

1   cup cream (half-and-
    half)
1   cup flour
2   eggs beaten separately
3   tablespoons melted
    shortening
½   teaspoon salt
2   teaspoons baking
    powder

Mix cream and flour and add egg yolks. Add shortening and salt. Fold in beaten egg whites and add baking powder just before cooking.

Makes about 5 waffles

Lucia Burke

65

BUTTERMILK PANCAKES

1   cup flour
2   cups buttermilk
2   eggs
1   teaspoon baking soda, dissolved in a little warm water

Whisk together the flour, buttermilk and eggs. Add baking soda and mix well. Cook on a lightly greased and very hot surface.

Serves 4

Ken Waterman

CUSTARD FRENCH TOAST

1   loaf French bread, cut in 1-inch slices
4   eggs
4   cups evaporated or whole milk
⅓   cup sugar
1   teaspoon vanilla
½   teaspoon salt
1   tablespoon sugar
2   teaspoons cinnamon

Divide bread slices and place in 2 greased rectangular glass baking dishes. Mix eggs, milk, ⅓ cup sugar, vanilla and salt. Pour over bread slices and refrigerate 12 hours. Bake at 325° for 30 to 45 minutes. Combine 1 tablespoon sugar and cinnamon and sprinkle over top before serving. Serve with syrup.

Serves 8

Kathy Daume

BASIC MUFFINS

¾ cup milk
⅓ cup salad oil
⅓ cup sugar
2 eggs
2 cups Bisquick mix

Combine milk, oil and sugar. Beat in eggs and add the Bisquick. Stir until well mixed. Mixture may be lumpy. Fill greased cupcake tins ⅔ full. Bake at 425° for 8 to 10 minutes.

1 cup of blueberries or other fruit may be added before baking.

Makes 12 muffins

BEER BREAD

3 cups self-rising flour
3 tablespoons sugar
1 can beer
1 stick butter, melted

Mix together flour, sugar and beer until well blended. Pour into a large loaf pan that has been well-greased. Drizzle butter over top of batter. Bake at 375° for 50 minutes.

Jeanne Edwards

BLUEBERRY MUFFINS

1 egg, beaten
1 cup milk
¼ cup butter, melted
2 cups flour
⅓ cup sugar
1 tablespoon baking powder
½ teaspoon salt
1 cup blueberries, rinsed and drained

Mix with a fork, egg, milk and butter. Sift together flour, sugar, baking powder and salt and combine with egg mixture. Fold in blueberries and spoon into well-greased muffin tins approximately ⅔ full. Bake at 425° for 20 minutes, until lightly browned.

Makes 10 to 12 muffins

BANANA BREAD

½   cup margarine
1   cup sugar
2   eggs
3   tablespoons buttermilk
2   large ripe bananas,
    mashed
2   cups flour
1   teaspoon baking soda
1   teaspoon baking powder
½   teaspoon salt
½   cup finely chopped nuts,
    optional

Cream margarine and sugar. Add eggs and dry ingredients followed by buttermilk, bananas and nuts. Bake for 1 hour at 325°.

Makes 2 medium-size loaves or two dozen muffins

Mom

BLUEBERRY BANANA BREAD

½   cup butter or margarine
1   cup sugar
2   eggs
1   cup mashed bananas
½   cup quick cooking oats,
     uncooked
1½   cups all-purpose flour
½   cup fresh blueberries
1   teaspoon baking soda
¼   teaspoon salt

Cream butter. Gradually add sugar; beat until light and fluffy. Add eggs one at a time, beating well after each. Stir in bananas. Combine remaining ingredients, stirring gently. Add blueberry mixture to creamed mixture. Bake in a well-greased and floured 9x5x3-inch loaf pan at 350° for 50 to 55 minutes. Cool in pan 10 minutes and then remove.

CAMILLE'S BISCUITS

4   cups Bisquick
1   8-ounce carton sour
     cream
¾   cup club soda
Melted butter

Mix all ingredients. Roll out thick and cut into biscuits. Brush with melted butter and bake at 400° for 10 to 12 minutes until brown.

Camille Murphey

BROCCOLI CORNBREAD

1½ sticks margarine, melted and cooled
1 medium onion, chopped
1 10-ounce package frozen, chopped broccoli, thawed
1 12-ounce carton small curd cottage cheese
4 eggs
2 boxes Jiffy cornbread mix

Mix all ingredients, then pour into a greased 9x13-inch pan. Bake at 350° for 30 to 40 minutes or until done.

CINNAMON ROLLS

1 can refrigerated crescent rolls
4 tablespoons melted butter
2 tablespoons sugar
2 tablespoons brown sugar
1 tablespoon honey
½ teaspoon cinnamon
½ cup raisins
½ cup chopped pecans , optional
Cinnamon sugar

Line a cookie sheet with aluminum foil and coat the foil with cooking spray. Separate rolls and place flat on cookie sheet. Combine remaining ingredients and spoon approximately 1 tablespoon of the mixture onto each of the 8 rolls. Fold each roll together, pinching ends to keep filling inside. Drizzle any remaining butter over the rolls. Sprinkle the tops with cinnamon sugar. Bake at 350° for 15 minutes or until rolls are lightly browned.

Serves 4

ANNE'S CINNAMON ROLLS

DOUGH

3 cups Pioneer dry biscuit mix
1 cup milk

Preheat oven to 325°. Lightly grease a 9x13-inch baking pan. Blend biscuit mix and milk. Knead 3 or 4 times. Roll dough to ¼-inch thickness. Fold dough into quarters. Roll dough into a 12x8-inch rectangle, ¼-inch thick.

FILLING

¾ cup butter melted, divided use
6 tablespoons sugar
2¼ teaspoons cinnamon
¾ cup raisins, optional
¾ cup pecans, chopped, optional

Spread dough with 3 tablespoons melted butter. Sprinkle with mixture of sugar and cinnamon. Allow butter to absorb sugar mixture. Roll dough from the long side and seal edges. Cut into 12 1-inch slices and place in prepared pan. Brush tops with ¼ cup additional butter and bake 25 to 30 minutes. When done, brush tops with remaining butter and drizzle with glaze.

GLAZE

1 cup powdered sugar
4 teaspoons milk
1 butter, melted
½ teaspoon vanilla

Combine all glaze ingredients and drizzle over cooked cinnamon rolls.

Serves 12

Anne DeuPree Duke

COFFEE CAKE

1 box butter cake mix
¾ cup sugar
½ cup vegetable oil
1 8-ounce carton sour
   cream
4 eggs
1 teaspoon almond
   extract
4 tablespoons brown
   sugar
2 teaspoons cinnamon
¾ cup raisins

ICING

1 cup powdered sugar
1 tablespoon butter,
   melted
1 tablespoon cream
1 teaspoon almond
   extract

Combine cake mix, sugar, oil and sour cream. Blend well. Add eggs, one at a time, beating well after each. Add almond extract. In a separate bowl, combine brown sugar, cinnamon and raisins together. Pour half of the batter in a greased bundt pan. Spoon brown sugar mixture evenly over the top of the batter layer. Cover with remainder of batter. Bake at 350° for about 1 hour or until tester comes out clean. Let cake stand for 15 minutes before removing from pan. While cake is still warm, drizzle the icing over the cake allowing it to run down the sides.

Mix all icing ingredients and drizzle over warm cake.

GARLIC OR SPINACH BREAD

1 cup mayonnaise
6 cloves garlic, minced
¾ cup grated Parmesan cheese
½ cup grated Cheddar cheese
1 tablespoon light cream
¼ teaspoon paprika
1 loaf French bread

Mix mayonnaise, garlic and Parmesan cheese in a small bowl. In a saucepan, melt Cheddar cheese, cream and paprika, stirring constantly. Blend mayonnaise mixture into cheese mixture. Cut French bread in half, lengthwise and toast lightly. Spread cheese on French bread. Broil in oven for 2 to 3 minutes until lightly browned.

This mixture will keep indefinitely in the refrigerator in an airtight container.

For spinach bread, add 1 package of frozen, chopped spinach which has been cooked according to package directions and well drained.

Serves 8

Sue Geren

MEXICAN CORNBREAD

2 eggs
1 cup chopped onion
1 tablespoon salt
1 tablespoon pepper
1 teaspoon baking soda
1 cup yellow cornmeal
1 cup grated Cheddar cheese
1 pound ground beef
1 cup buttermilk
2 jalapeño peppers, seeded and chopped
1 small can cream style corn

Sauté onions and beef. In a separate large mixing bowl, combine cornmeal and cheese. Add all other ingredients. Place in a greased 9x9-inch baking dish. Bake at 375° for 45 minutes.

Serves 6 to 8

Marti Clinesmith

POPPY SEED MUFFINS

¼ cup poppy seeds
⅔ cup salad oil
1   box yellow cake mix
1   3-ounce package
    coconut cream pudding
⅔ cup water
4   eggs
½ teaspoon almond
    extract

Mix poppy seeds in oil. Blend cake mix, pudding, water and oil with poppy seeds in mixer at medium speed. Add eggs, one at a time, blending thoroughly after each. Add extract. Pour batter into greased muffin tins. Bake at 350° for 35 minutes. Batter may also be used for a cake. Simply pour batter into a greased and floured tube or bundt pan. Bake cake at same temperature for 1 hour.

PUMPKIN BREAD

1   cup vegetable oil
3   cups sugar
3   eggs, beaten
1   15-ounce can pumpkin
3   cups flour
1   teaspoon cloves
1   teaspoon nutmeg
1   teaspoon cinnamon
1   teaspoon baking soda
½ teaspoon salt
¾ teaspoon baking
    powder

Combine oil and sugar and mix well. Add beaten eggs and pumpkin. Sift dry ingredients and add to pumpkin mixture. Pour into three greased and floured loaf pans. Bake for 1 hour at 350°.

Makes 3 loaves

Jeanne Edwards

STRAWBERRY BREAD

3   cups flour
2   cups sugar
1   teaspoon salt
1   teaspoon soda
½   teaspoon cinnamon
1   16-ounce package
    unsweetened frozen
    strawberries, thawed
½   cup vegetable oil
4   eggs, beaten
1½ cups chopped nuts,
    optional

In a large bowl, sift together flour, sugar, salt, soda and cinnamon. In another bowl, combine strawberries, oil, eggs and nuts. Add liquid ingredients gradually to dry ingredients, mixing well. Line two 8x4-inch loaf pans with foil and pour batter into pans. Bake at 325° for 1 hour or until done.

Makes 2 loaves

STRAWBERRY-BANANA BREAD

1½ cups sifted flour
2½ cups sugar
2   teaspoons baking
    powder
½   teaspoon salt
¾   cup quick-cooking oats
⅓   cup salad oil
2   eggs, slightly beaten
1   cup whole strawberries,
    mashed to ½ cup
1   medium banana,
    mashed

Sift flour, sugar, baking powder and salt. Stir in oats. Add oil, eggs, strawberries and banana, stirring until no dry ingredients show. Put in a greased loaf pan and bake at 350° until tester comes out clean - about 1 hour.

May also be baked as muffins.

Makes 1 loaf

ZUCCHINI BREAD

3   eggs
¾   cup cooking oil
2   cups sugar
2   cups raw, grated
    zucchini
2   teaspoons vanilla
3   cups flour
1   teaspoon baking soda
½   teaspoon baking
    powder
1   teaspoon cinnamon
½   cup chopped nuts,
    optional

Beat eggs and add oil. Mix well. Add sugar, zucchini and vanilla and beat until well blended. Add remaining ingredients and mix thoroughly. Pour into 2 greased loaf pans and bake at 350° for about 1 hour.

May also be made as muffins.

Makes 2 loaves

BLENDER HOLLANDAISE

3   egg yolks
1-2   tablespoons lemon
    juice
¼   teaspoon salt
Dash of cayenne pepper
½   cup butter, melted

Blend egg yolks, lemon juice salt and cayenne on high speed. Slowly add melted butter. Sauce will keep at room temperature for an hour before serving.

Makes 1 cup

Sue Geren

EASY HOLLANDAISE SAUCE

1   egg yolk, slightly
    beaten
1-1½   tablespoons lemon
    juice
½   stick cold butter
Salt to taste
White pepper to taste

Place all ingredients in a saucepan. Cook over low heat, stirring constantly until butter melts and sauce is thickened.

Makes ½ cup

Vegetables

EASY FRESH ASPARAGUS

Fresh asparagus (as much as desired)
Squeeze margarine
Garlic salt to taste
Pepper to taste

Wash asparagus and snap off tough ends. Arrange in a rectangular baking dish. Add enough water to moisten the bottom of the dish. Squeeze margarine over the asparagus and season. Bake at 350° until bright green and semi-tender - about 10 minutes.

ASPARAGUS VENETIAN

2 **pounds fresh asparagus, cooked until barely tender**
1 **package dried onion soup mix**
½ **pound butter, melted**
1 **cup mozzarella cheese, grated**
2 **tablespoons grated Parmesan cheese**

Combine butter and onion soup mix. Arrange asparagus in rectangular baking dish (use cooking spray). Pour butter mixture over asparagus. Sprinkle cheeses on top. Bake 10 minutes at 450°.

Serves 4 to 6

Marti Clinesmith

PIÑON NUT BARLEY BAKE

½ **cup sliced mushrooms**
½ **cup chopped green onions**
5 **tablespoons margarine**
1 **cup barley**
⅓ **cup chopped parsley**
2-3 **cups chicken broth**
½ **cup pine nuts**
Salt and pepper

Sauté mushrooms and onion in margarine. Add barley and cook until golden in color. In a 2-quart casserole (use cooking spray), combine barley, parsley and 1 cup of chicken broth. Bake uncovered at 350°. After 30 minutes, stir in pine nuts and 1 cup of chicken broth. Bake uncovered another 45 minutes. Add more broth as needed.

Serves 4 to 6

Jean Finch

BAKED BEANS

1 large can pork & beans
2 strips bacon, diced
1 medium onion, chopped
1 medium green pepper, chopped
1 teaspoon chili powder
½ teaspoon salt
2 tablespoons brown sugar
½ cup ketchup

Mix all ingredients well and place in greased casserole. Bake for 1 hour at 350°. May be made ahead and baked just before serving.

Serves 8

EPISCOPAL GREEN BEANS

2 16-ounce cans whole green beans
Garlic salt to taste
1 stick butter or margarine, melted
2 tablespoons prepared mustard
2 tablespoons Worcestershire sauce

Drain half the liquid from beans. Place beans and remaining liquid in a saucepan and season generously with garlic salt. Cook on medium heat about 20 minutes and then drain. Combine butter, Worcestershire and mustard and add to beans. Marinate 6 to 12 hours. Reheat before serving.

Serves 6 to 8

Sue Geren

GARLIC GREEN BEANS

1-2 pounds green beans (as desired)
4 tablespoons butter
Garlic salt

Wash and trim green beans. Sauté in skillet with butter and garlic salt to taste until tender but still crisp.

May substitute fresh minced garlic and salt to taste

Sue Geren

79

GREEN BEAN BUNDLES

2   cans vertical packed green beans
½   pound bacon
½   cup butter
½   cup brown sugar
1½ teaspoons garlic salt

Drain beans and divide into bundles of approximately 5 beans each. Wrap each bundle with half a slice of bacon. Secure with a toothpick if necessary. Place bundles in a well-greased shallow baking dish. Melt butter and sugar together and add garlic salt. Pour mixture over the beans and bake for 30 to 45 minutes at 350°. May be made the night before and baked before serving.

Serves 8

MARTI'S GREEN BEANS

2   cans cut green beans
3   bacon slices, browned and in small pieces
Garlic salt to taste
Pepper to taste

Simmer all of the above until as we say, all nutritional value is gone!

Serves 4 to 6

Marti Clinesmith

COMPANY CAULIFLOWER

1 head cauliflower
1 8-ounce carton sour cream
½ cup grated Cheddar cheese
3 tablespoons toasted sesame seeds

Break cauliflower into florets. Cook and drain. Place half the cauliflower in a well-greased 1½-quart casserole. Spread half the sour cream and half the cheese on top. Repeat the layers. Sprinkle with sesame seeds. Bake at 350° for 10 minutes or until cheese melts.

Serves 4 to 6

BROCCOLI CASSEROLE

2   10-ounce packages
    frozen chopped
    broccoli
1   can cream of mushroom
    soup
1   egg
1   cup grated Cheddar
    cheese
1   cup mayonnaise
¾   cup onion, chopped
1   teaspoon salt
½   teaspoon pepper

Cook broccoli according to package directions until tender. In a bowl, combine all other ingredients and mix well. Add the drained chopped broccoli and mix well. Pour into greased baking dish. Bake at 350° for 30 to 45 minutes or until bubbly around the edges.

May be made ahead and frozen or refrigerated until ready to cook.

Serves 6 to 8

GLAZED CARROTS

1   16-ounce package
    frozen baby carrots
4   tablespoons butter
4   tablespoons brown
    sugar
1   tablespoon orange juice
½   teaspoon salt

Cook carrots according to package directions. Drain and add all other ingredients. Heat thoroughly.

Serves 6 to 8

Donna's Corn Casserole

2 cans white shoe peg corn, drained
1 8-ounce package cream cheese, softened
¼ cup milk
1 stick butter, softened
1 small can chopped green chilies
Garlic salt
Pepper
Dash of Tabasco
Grated Cheddar cheese

Combine all ingredients, placing cheese on top. Bake in a well-greased casserole at 350° for 30 to 40 minutes. Chopped jalapeños may be used for extra spiciness.

Serves 6 to 8

Donna Kohler

Corn Pudding

¼ stick margarine
1 16-ounce can creamed corn
2 tablespoons sugar
1 heaping tablespoon flour
Salt and pepper to taste
2 eggs
1 5-ounce can evaporated milk

Melt margarine in a 1½-quart casserole that has been coated with cooking spray. Pour corn into casserole and add sugar, flour and seasonings. Stir in eggs and milk. Mix well. Bake at 350° for 1 hour or until knife inserted in center comes out clean.

Serves 6

CORNBREAD DRESSING

3 packages Jiffy
   cornbread mix
1 package Pepperidge
   Farm dry dressing mix
5 eggs, beaten
4 cans chicken broth
Salt and pepper
2 large onion, chopped
2 sticks butter
1 teaspoon sage

Prepare cornbread according to package a day or two before assembling the dressing. Sauté onions in 1 stick butter. In a large container, crumble cornbread and add dry dressing mix. Add eggs, chicken broth (3 cans), onions and seasoning to taste. Dressing should be soupy. If not, add more broth. Seal container and let sit at least overnight. To bake, place dressing in a well-greased 9x13-inch pan or a roasting pan. Drizzle 1 stick of melted butter and half of a can of chicken broth over the top and bake at 350° for 45 to 60 minutes. Dressing should not be overcooked as it will be too dry. It is done when firm and lightly golden brown.

Serves 8 to 10

Vers

BAKED EGGPLANT

1 large eggplant, cooked
2 eggs, beaten
15-20 saltine crackers, crushed
1 small can evaporated
   milk
Dash of hot sauce
Salt and pepper to taste
2 tablespoons melted
   margarine
½ cups sharp yellow
   cheese, grated
1 small onion, diced

Mash eggplant and mix remaining ingredients. Pour into greased casserole. Can be topped with additional grated cheese. Bake at 350° for 25 to 30 minutes until set.

Yellow squash and zucchini can be substituted for eggplant.

Serves 6 to 8

Grace DeuPree

ADULT MACARONI & CHEESE

1 box macaroni & cheese
1 4.5-ounce can chopped
   green chilies
2 heaping tablespoons
   sour cream
1 small jar chopped
   pimentos, optional

Prepare macaroni and cheese according to directions on box. Add rest of ingredients and place in covered 2-quart casserole (use cooking spray). Bake at 350° for 30 minutes.

Serves 6

Mom

ONION CASSEROLE

1 package frozen small
   white onions
3 tablespoons butter
1 can cream of mushroom
   soup
½ cup chopped almonds
¼ cup half and half
Grated cheese, if desired

Cook onions in boiling salted water until barely tender. Drain. Place onions in a casserole and dot with butter. In a separate mixing bowl, combine soup, almonds and cream. Pour over onions. Cover with grated cheese. Bake at 350° for 30 minutes.

Serves 4 to 6

Lucile Finch

MAMA SUE'S ONION CASSEROLE

12 medium onions, thinly
   sliced
1 large bag potato chips,
   crushed
½ pound mild Cheddar
   cheese, grated
2 cans cream of
   mushroom soup
½ cup milk
⅛ teaspoon cayenne
   pepper or to taste

In a buttered 9x13-inch casserole place alternate layers of onions, chips and cheese. Mix mushroom soup and milk. Pour over onion mixture, it will cook through. Sprinkle cayenne pepper over top and bake at 350° for 1 hour.

Great with steaks and barbecue!

Serves 8 to 10

Sue Geren

CHEESE ONION SQUARES

10 ounces sharp Cheddar
   cheese, grated
12 ounces frozen diced
   onions
3 cups Bisquick
2 cups milk
2 eggs
2 tablespoons butter or
   margarine
4 teaspoons butter or
   margarine, melted
Poppy seeds

Sauté onions in 2 tablespoons butter until transparent. Mix Bisquick, eggs, milk, half of cheese and onions. Grease 9x13-inch Pyrex pan and pour in mixture. Sprinkle with the other half of cheese, melted butter and lots of poppy seeds. Bake at 400° for 25 to 30 minutes until set. Cut into serving size portions.

May be frozen and reheated in foil with top open.

Cut in bite size pieces and serve as an appetizer.

Serves 10 to 12

Kathy Daume

CREAMED ONIONS

2 14.5-ounce jars onions, drained, reserve liquid
6 tablespoons butter
6 tablespoons flour
2 cups milk
1 tablespoon sour cream
½ teaspoon garlic salt
¼ teaspoon pepper
1 teaspoon Worcestershire sauce
1 tablespoon grated Parmesan cheese

In a large saucepan melt butter. Add flour and blend until smooth. Add milk slowly, stirring constantly. As sauce thickens, add sour cream. When sauce is thickened, add seasonings and cheese. Add drained onions and heat through. If sauce is too thick, simply add a little of the reserved onion liquid.

Fresh pearl onions may be substituted. Simply peel and boil until tender before adding to the cream sauce.

Serves 6 to 8

Mom

DELICIOUS BLACK-EYED PEAS

1 pound dried black-eyed peas
1 tablespoon salt
1 clove garlic, cut in half
2 ham hocks
3 cloves garlic, minced
2 onions, chopped
1 green pepper, chopped
2 bay leaves
2 tablespoons bacon grease
1 teaspoon salt
Pepper

Wash peas. Put peas in a Dutch oven, cover with water and soak overnight. Drain peas and cover with fresh water. Add 1 tablespoon salt, garlic halves and ham hocks. Cover and simmer 2 hours, adding water as needed. In a skillet, cook minced garlic, onion and green pepper in bacon grease until soft. Add vegetables and bay leaves to peas with 1 teaspoon salt and pepper to taste. Simmer 1 hour.

Add 1 pound sliced and browned Polish sausage during last hour of cooking.

Freezes well.

Serves 10

CHUCK'S BLACK-EYED PEAS

2 15.5-ounce cans Jalapeño black-eyed peas
1 can Rotel tomatoes
1 14.5-ounce can tomatoes, diced
1 pound pork sausage
1 tablespoon oil
1 medium onion, chopped
1 green pepper, chopped
1 jalapeño, chopped, optional
⅔ cup raw white rice

Sauté onion, green pepper and jalapeño in oil until tender. Add sausage and cook until done. Drain off grease and put mixture in a large soup pot. Add rice, peas and tomatoes with juice. Simmer until rice is cooked, about 30 minutes.

Serve with cornbread.

Serves 8

Chuck Cerf

87

BAKED POTATO CASSEROLE

4   baking potatoes, boiled
     until tender
1½ cups light cream
1   stick butter
½   pound grated Cheddar
     cheese
1   8-ounce carton sour
     cream
½   cup chopped green
     onions
6   strips bacon, fried and
     crumbled

Peel cooled potatoes and grate. Combine cream, butter, and cheese and heat until all cheese has melted. Add cheese mixture to grated potatoes and put in a greased 9x13-inch casserole. Bake at 350° for about 30 minutes or until bubbly. Top with sour cream, onions, and bacon. Bake about 5 minutes.

Serves 8

MAKE AHEAD MASHED POTATOES

8-10 potatoes, peeled
1   8 ounce package cream
     cheese, softened
1   cup sour cream
2   tablespoons chopped
     chives
Salt and pepper
4   tablespoons butter

Quarter the potatoes and boil in salted water until soft in the centers. Drain. Whip the hot potatoes, adding the cream cheese and sour cream. Continue beating until fluffy and smooth. Add chives, salt and pepper to taste. Place in a well-greased 9x13-inch baking dish. Dot top of potatoes with butter. Cover with foil and refrigerate. Bake covered casserole at 325° for 15 minutes. Remove cover and continue baking 20 minutes or until crusty on top.

Serves 10 to 12

Nancy Kendzior

BLENDER POTATOES

½ cup milk
3 eggs
½ teaspoon salt
⅛ teaspoon pepper
1 cup cubed processed
   American cheese
2 tablespoons butter
½ onion, chopped
3 medium potatoes,
   peeled and cubed

Place all ingredients in blender in the order listed. Cover and blend on high speed until all potatoes are grated. Do not over blend. Pour into well-greased 10x6x1½-inch baking dish. Bake for 35 to 40 minutes at 350°.

Serves 6

CHEESY NEW POTATOES

12 medium new potatoes
2 cups grated Cheddar
   cheese
16 slices bacon, fried crisp
   and crumbled
½ cup butter, melted
Salt and pepper

Wash and cube potatoes. Do not peel. Cook in boiling water until just barely tender. Remove from heat and drain. Season to taste. In a large casserole place a layer of potatoes, half the bacon, half the butter and half the cheese. Repeat the layers. Heat at 350° for 20 to 30 minutes.

Serves 8 to 10

POTATOES AND ONIONS

6 new potatoes, sliced
   with skins
2 onions, sliced
1 stick butter
Salt
Pepper

Melt half the stick of butter in a large skillet. Add a layer of potatoes followed by a layer of onions. Season and add 1 or 2 more tablespoons of butter. Repeat the layers. Cook over medium heat until potatoes are cooked through. Stir to brown evenly.

Serves 4

Sue Geren

HASH BROWN CASSEROLE

1   32-ounce package frozen hash brown potatoes (not shredded), thawed
1   can cream of chicken soup
2   sticks of butter
1   8-ounce carton of sour cream
12   ounces grated American cheese
1   medium onion, chopped
1   teaspoon salt
2   cups corn flakes, crushed

In a 13x9-inch casserole, put thawed hash browns, chopped onion, and mix well. Mix together soup, sour cream, cheese and one stick of melted butter. Spread this over potatoes. Top with crushed corn flakes and then drizzle the other stick of butter on top. Bake for 45 minutes at 350°.

Serves 8

Nancy Zally

ONION-ROASTED POTATOES

1   package dry onion soup
2   pounds potatoes (peeled and cut into large chunks)
⅓   cup olive or vegetable oil

Preheat oven to 450°. In a large plastic bag or bowl, add all ingredients. Close bag and shake, or toss in bowl, until potatoes are evenly coated. Place in well-greased shallow baking or roasting pan. Bake, stirring occasionally, 40 minutes or until potatoes are tender and golden brown.

Serves 6 to 8

CANDIED SWEET POTATOES

6	sweet potatoes, medium size (about 4½ pounds)
⅓	cup brown sugar, firmly packed
½	cup sugar
2	tablespoons flour
1	teaspoon cinnamon
¼	teaspoon nutmeg
¼	teaspoon allspice
¾	cup pineapple juice
2	tablespoons orange juice
¼	cup butter
½	cup pecans, chopped

Preheat oven to 350°. Cook potatoes until tender. Let cool to touch then peel and cut lengthwise into ¼-inch slices. Set aside. Combine brown sugar, sugar, flour, cinnamon, nutmeg, and allspice in a saucepan, stir in juices and butter. Cook over medium heat for about 10 minutes, stirring often. Place half of potatoes in lightly greased 13x9x2-inch pan. Pour half of sugar mixture over potatoes; repeat layer. Sprinkle with pecans and bake about 30 minutes until bubbly.

Serves 8

Anne DeuPree Duke

SWEET POTATO SOUFFLÉ

2	cups mashed sweet potatoes or 1 (29-ounce) can, drained
1	cup sugar
2	eggs
¾	stick butter
½	cup milk
½	teaspoon nutmeg
½	teaspoon cinnamon

Mix sweet potatoes, sugar, eggs, butter, milk, and spices well. Pour into a buttered soufflé dish. Bake at 400° for 20 minutes.

TOPPING

¾	cup crushed corn flakes or graham crackers
½	cup chopped pecans, optional
½	cup light brown sugar, tightly packed
¾	stick butter

Topping: Melt butter. Add remaining ingredients; mix well. Cover sweet potatoes with topping. Return to oven for 10 additional minutes.

Serves 6 to 8

CHINESE FRIED RICE

10 slices bacon
3 tablespoons bacon drippings
½ cup chopped green onions
1 cup sliced mushrooms
2½ cups cooked white rice
2 tablespoons soy sauce
1 egg, beaten

Fry bacon until crisp, drain and crumble. Reserve 3 tablespoons bacon drippings. Add onion to drippings and cook until almost tender. Add mushrooms, rice and soy sauce. Reduce heat and simmer about 10 minutes, stirring occasionally. Stir egg into rice mixture and cook only until egg is done. Sprinkle bacon over top of rice.

Serves 8

GREEN CHILI RICE

3 cups sour cream
1 cup chopped green chilies
3 cups cooked rice
Salt and pepper to taste
¾ pound Monterey Jack Cheese

Mix sour cream, chilies, salt and pepper. Add cooked rice. Place half of the rice mixture in the bottom of a greased round casserole. Top with half of the cheese. Repeat. Bake at 350° for about 25 minutes or until the cheese is melted and bubbly.

May be made ahead and baked before serving.

Serves 6 to 8

PERFECT RICE

2 cups long grain rice
  (not Minute Rice or
  converted)
3 cups cold water
2 teaspoons salt

Wash rice, drain and place in a heavy 4-quart saucepan with water and salt. Bring to a hard boil, stir once and cover tightly. Reduce heat to low and cook about 30 minutes. Do Not lift cover during cooking. Liquid will be completely absorbed when rice is done. Remove from heat and fluff with a fork.

Yields 6 cups

Sue Geren

RICE CASSEROLE

1 stick butter
1 can beef consommé
1 can French onion soup
1 4.5-ounce jar
  mushrooms, drained, or
  ½ cup fresh mushrooms
¼ cup slivered almonds,
  optional
1 cup white rice

Melt butter in a greased casserole. Add all other ingredients and bake at 350° for approximately 45 minutes or until rice is tender.

Serves 6

Nancy Carter Mason

RICE PILAF

1 can mushrooms,
  drained
¼ pound butter
1 teaspoon oregano
2 cups raw white rice
8-10 green onions, chopped
3 cans beef consommé
2 cans water

Sauté mushrooms in butter. Add oregano, rice, onions and brown. Place in a 3-quart casserole (use cooking spray). Add consommé and water. Cover and bake at 450° for 1 hour.

Serves 8 to 10

Frances Templeton

RICE O'MURPHY

1 cup raw rice
2 cups water
3 chicken bouillon cubes
1 teaspoon salt
¼ cup butter
½ cup sliced green onions
½ cup diced green pepper
3 tablespoons pimento
½ cup chopped ripe olives

Dissolve bouillon in water. Bring to a boil and add rice and salt. Cook covered until done. Heat butter in skillet and add cooked rice, green onions, and green peppers. Sauté until vegetables are tender and crisp. Fork toss with pimento and olives.

Serves 6

Betsy Murphy

CREAMED SPINACH

½ stick butter or margarine
2 10-ounce packages chopped spinach
Garlic salt
Pepper
1 cup sour cream

Melt butter in skillet. Add spinach and cook until done. Season to taste and add sour cream. Heat thoroughly.

Serves 6

CREAMED SPINACH CASSEROLE

3 packages frozen chopped spinach
1 8-ounce package cream cheese
2 eggs, separated
1 can cream of mushroom soup
4 tablespoons Parmesan cheese
1 can French fried onion rings

Cook and drain spinach. Beat egg yolks. Heat soup and cream cheese. Add egg yolks and mix well. Add spinach, beaten egg whites and Parmesan cheese. Put in greased casserole dish and top with onion rings. Bake at 350° for 35 to 45 minutes.

Serves 10

JALAPEÑO SPINACH

½ large onion, chopped
1 6-ounce jar mushroom slices, drained
5 tablespoons margarine or buttered, divided
1 10-ounce package frozen chopped spinach, slightly thawed
Garlic salt to taste
1 8-ounce package jalapeño cheese
1 can cream of mushroom soup

Sauté onion and mushrooms in 3 tablespoons of butter or margarine. Drain and set aside. Cook spinach in remaining 2 tablespoons of butter until no water is left in pan. Season with garlic salt. Add soup, cheese, and sautéed vegetables. Allow soup to melt and put in baking dish. Bake at 350° until hot. This may be prepared ahead of time and simply baked prior to serving.

Serves 6 to 8

QUICK JALAPEÑO SPINACH

1 10-ounce package frozen chopped spinach
1 8-ounce package jalapeño cheese
2 tablespoons butter or margarine
Garlic salt to taste

Cook spinach in butter or margarine until no water is left in pan. Season with garlic salt. Add jalapeño cheese and allow to melt.

Serves 4

SPINACH CASSEROLE

1 10-ounce package frozen chopped spinach
1 8-ounce package cream cheese
2 tablespoons butter, softened
⅛ teaspoon garlic salt
Pepper to taste
1½ cups Parmesan cheese

Cook spinach according to directions and drain well. Mix spinach with cream cheese, butter and salt. Put into a casserole coated with cooking spray and cover with Parmesan cheese. Bake at 350° for 30 minutes or until cheese melts.

Serves 6

SPINACH SOUFFLÉ

1   10-ounce package
    frozen chopped spinach
1   can cream of mushroom
    soup
½   cup mayonnaise
¼   cup chopped onion
3   eggs

Cook spinach according to directions until thawed. Drain well. Add onions. Beat eggs well and gradually add soup and mayonnaise to eggs. Combine spinach and soup mixture. Bake in a greased soufflé dish at 350° for 40 minutes or until set and lightly browned.

Serves 6 to 8

SPINACH SOUFFLÉ #2

1   10-ounce package
    frozen chopped
    spinach, thawed
½   cup cream
1   8-ounce package cream
    cheese, cubed
5   eggs
½   cup plus 1 tablespoon
    grated Parmesan cheese
½   teaspoon garlic salt
½   teaspoon white pepper
Pinch of nutmeg

In a strainer, remove excess moisture from spinach. Place all ingredients, except 1 tablespoon Parmesan cheese, in a blender or food processor. Blend until thoroughly combined. Butter a 1½-quart soufflé dish. Sprinkle with remaining cheese. Pour mixture into prepared dish and bake at 375° for 50 minutes or until puffed and golden.

Serves 6

SPINACH SOUFFLÉ #3

3 tablespoons butter
¼ cup flour
1 teaspoon garlic salt
¼ teaspoon white pepper
⅛ teaspoon nutmeg
1 cup half and half
1 cup Swiss cheese, grated
1 10-ounce package frozen chopped spinach, thawed and drained
4 eggs, separated

In a medium saucepan, melt butter and blend in flour, salt, pepper, and nutmeg. Gradually add cream, stirring until well blended. Cook over low heat, stirring constantly, until thick and smooth. Add cheese and drained spinach and continue cooking until cheese is melted. Cool. In a separate bowls, beat egg whites until stiff and the yolk until thick and bright yellow. Add yolks to spinach. Fold in egg whites. Pour into buttered 1½-quart soufflé dish. Bake at 325° for 45 to 50 minutes. Serve immediately.

Serves 4 to 6

BAKED ACORN SQUASH

3 acorn squash
¼ cup butter or margarine, melted
⅓ cup brown sugar
1 teaspoon cinnamon
½ teaspoon salt
½ teaspoon ginger

Slice squash in half, lengthwise. Scoop out seeds. Place squash halves in a greased baking dish cut side down and bake at 350° for 30 to 40 minutes, until tender. Remove from oven and turn squash to cut side up. Combine remaining ingredients and pour inside squash. Continue baking for 15 minutes or until glaze begins to brown.

Serves 6

Stuffed Squash

8	large yellow squash
1	onion, chopped fine
¾	stick butter
1	rib celery, chopped fine, optional
⅔	cup seasoned Italian bread crumbs
⅓	roll jalapeño cheese
1	egg

Boil squash in water until tender, about 20 minutes. Drain and carefully place squash on a paper towel. While still hot, cut in half. Scoop out inside of squash into a bowl containing the cheese which has been cut into small pieces. To this mixture add slightly beaten egg and bread crumbs. In a large skillet sauté onion and celery until tender, but not brown. Add squash mixture and salt to taste. Cook slowly stirring often for 20 to 25 minutes. Stuff squash halves with this mixture. Top each squash with a pat of butter and ½ teaspoon of bread crumbs. Bake at 350° for 20 to 25 minutes.

Freezes well. Do not top with butter or crumbs if freezing. Add before baking, when thawed.

May substitute finely chopped green onions for onion.

Serves 8 to 10

Sue Geren

Baked Squash

3	cups yellow squash, grated
3	eggs, slightly beaten
¼	cup milk
¼	cup butter, melted
1	teaspoon salt
¼	teaspoon pepper
½	cup bread crumbs

Cook squash in a small amount of water until tender. Drain well. Combine all other ingredients except the bread crumbs and fold in squash. Pour into a greased casserole and top with bread crumbs. Bake at 350° for 45 minutes.

Serves 4

SCALLOPED SUMMER SQUASH

3 tablespoons butter
1 medium onion, minced
1 clove garlic, minced
1 green pepper, finely chopped
4 medium tomatoes, peeled and chopped
Salt and pepper to taste
1½ pounds summer squash, sliced or cubed
1 cup grated Parmesan cheese

In a medium skillet, melt butter. Add onion, garlic and green pepper. Sauté until tender. Add the tomatoes and seasonings and simmer, stirring occasionally. Cook squash in boiling water until just tender. Drain well. Lightly coat a deep casserole with cooking spray. Add half of the squash. Pour half of the tomato mixture over the squash. Sprinkle tomatoes with half of the cheese. Repeat the layers, ending with cheese. Bake at 350° until cheese topping is bubbly.

Serves 6

Mary Styron

ZUCCHINI SOUFFLÉ

2 eggs, beaten
1 cup mayonnaise
½ cup chopped onion
1 cup Parmesan cheese
4 cups grated zucchini, par boiled

Combine first four ingredients and add drained zucchini. Place in 1½-quart greased round casserole. Bake at 350° for 30 to 35 minutes.

Serves 6

Tomato Tart

1   9-inch pie crust
1   tablespoon Parmesan
    cheese
5   medium to large
    tomatoes, sliced
Salt to taste
Pepper to taste
½   teaspoon oregano
1   cup chopped, green
    onions
1   cup mayonnaise
2   cups sharp Cheddar
    cheese, grated
½   cup Parmesan cheese
2   small tomatoes, thinly
    sliced

Drain tomatoes on paper towels for 15 minutes. Preheat oven to 350°. Sprinkle bottom of crust with 1 tablespoon of Parmesan cheese. Cover with 2 layers of tomatoes. Sprinkle with salt, pepper, oregano, 1.2 cup onion. Repeat layers. Mix mayonnaise and Cheddar cheese. Spread over layers. Top with Parmesan cheese. Decorate top with sliced, small tomatoes. Bake 50 minutes. Serve at room temperature.

Serves 6 to 8

Kathy Daume

Entrées

BEEF TENDERLOIN

3-4 **pound beef tenderloin**
Garlic pepper
2 **tablespoons**
Worcestershire sauce
½ **cup Wishbone Italian**
Dressing

Place tenderloin in roasting pan. Sprinkle heavily with garlic pepper. Pour Worcestershire sauce and Italian dressing over tenderloin and allow to come to room temperature. Preheat oven to 500°. Place in hot oven and cook for 5 minutes. Reduce the oven temperature to 350°; bake for 15 additional minutes or until meat thermometer registers 120° (for rare). Meat will continue to cook after removing from oven.

Sue Geren

BETSY'S BRISKET

1 **whole brisket**
1 **12-ounce jar chili sauce**
1 **can cola, not diet**
1 **package dry onion soup**
mix

Line roasting pan with enough aluminum foil to completely cover meat. Score fat side of meat to show grain and place in pan, fat side up. In a separate bowl, mix chili sauce, cola and soup. Pour over brisket. Seal meat with foil. Bake at 325° for 3 to 5 hours. Cool. When ready to serve, slice meat against the grain. Refrigerate sauce from pan. Remove fat from sauce. To reheat, pour sauce over sliced brisket and heat at 350° for 30 minutes. Again, cover pan with foil when reheating.

Betsy Murphy

MOCK BEEF BOURGUIGNONNE

2 pounds lean stew meat
1 cup red wine
1 4-ounce can mushrooms with juice
1 package dry onion soup mix
1 can cream of mushroom soup

Place all of the ingredients into a Dutch oven (use cooking spray.) Stir and cover. Place in a 300° oven for 3 hours. Do not stir or peek.

Serves 6 to 8

Jonnie Burke

BEEF CASSEROLE

1 pound ground beef
2 teaspoons salt
2 teaspoons sugar
1 16-ounce can chopped tomatoes
1 8-ounce can tomato sauce
½ teaspoon garlic puree
Pepper to taste
1 8-ounce carton sour cream
1 5-ounce package egg noodles, cooked and drained
1 3-ounce package cream cheese, softened
3 green onions, chopped
1 cup Cheddar cheese, grated

Brown beef in a large skillet and add salt, sugar, tomatoes, tomato sauce, garlic and pepper. Cook over low heat 5 to 10 minutes. Combine noodles with sour cream, cream cheese and green onions. In a greased 3-quart casserole arrange a layer of meat mixture and then a layer of noodle mixture. Repeat. Top with grated cheese. Bake at 350° for 35 minutes.

May be made ahead even the night before and refrigerated. Bake before serving.

Serves 6 to 8

103

BEEF STEW

2   **pounds top sirloin,
    cut in 1½-inch cubes**
⅓   **cup flour**
2   **teaspoons salt**
¼   **teaspoon pepper**
5   **slices bacon**
1   **clove garlic, crushed**
1   **cup beef consommé**
1   **cup burgundy wine**
2   **tablespoons chopped
    parsley**
3   **whole cloves**
Pinch of thyme
1   **bay leaf, crumbled**
2½   **cups carrots,
    cut in 1-inch pieces**
12   **small boiling onions**

Dredge beef with seasoned flour. Cook bacon in heavy kettle or soup pan until brown. Remove from pan, drain and crumble. Brown beef in bacon drippings with garlic. Add bacon, consommé, wine and parsley. Season with cloves, thyme and bay leaf. Cover and simmer 2 to 2½ hours or until meat is tender. Stir occasionally. If gravy becomes too thick, add water. Add carrots and onions and continue cooking, covered, for about 20 minutes or until vegetables are tender.

Serves 4 to 6

Nancy Kendzior

BEEF STROGANOFF

1½   **pounds top round steak
    cut into strips**
2   **tablespoons butter**
½   **pound fresh
    mushrooms, sliced**
½   **cup onion, minced**
1   **can beef consommé**
1   **teaspoon garlic salt**
3   **tablespoons flour**
1   **8-ounce carton sour
    cream**

Sauté mushrooms and onion in butter. Add beef and brown. Season mixture with garlic salt and add ⅔ of consommé. Cover and simmer 15 minutes. Add remaining consommé and flour. Stir constantly for one minute. Reduce heat and add sour cream. Serve over rice or noodles.

May be made the night before and reheated before serving.

Serves 4 to 6

HOT CHILI SOUP

1   3-pound can pinto beans
2   pounds ground chuck
1   red onion, chopped
1   clove garlic, minced
1   green pepper, chopped
3   4.5 ounce cans chopped green chilies
1   16-ounce can tomatoes, diced
¼   cup chili powder
2   tablespoons cumin
2   tablespoons hot red pepper sauce
2   teaspoons salt
4   tablespoons tomato paste
5   cups water
¼   cup picante sauce
Dash of cayenne pepper

Brown meat. Drain well. Add onion, garlic, green pepper and green chilies. Sauté until the onion is clear and add canned tomatoes. Turn burner off. In a large soup pot put beans, chili powder, cumin, pepper sauce, salt, tomato paste, water, picante and cayenne pepper. Heat. As bean mixture begins to boil, add beef mixture. Turn heat down and let chili simmer, covered, for 30 minutes and then uncovered for another 30 minutes.

Freezes well

Serves 8 to 10

COUNTRY PIE

2   8-ounce cans tomato sauce
½   cup bread crumbs
1   pound ground chuck
¼   cup onion, chopped
¼   cup green pepper, chopped
1½   teaspoon oregano
⅛   teaspoon pepper
½   teaspoon salt
1⅓   cups instant rice
1   cup water
1   cup grated Cheddar cheese, divided use

Combine ½ cup tomato sauce, bread crumbs, ground meat, onion and green pepper. Mix well. Pat meat mixture on the bottom and sides of a deep dish 9-inch pie plate. Combine rice, water, remainder of tomato sauce, ¼ cup cheese, salt and pepper. Spoon over meat mixture. Cover with aluminum foil and bake at 350° for 25 minutes. Uncover and sprinkle with remaining cheese. Bake an additional 10 to 15 minutes.

Serves 6

ENCHILADA CASSEROLE

1 cup water
¼ cup + 2 tablespoons picante sauce, divided
12 corn tortillas
2 pounds ground beef
1 onion, chopped
1 teaspoon salt
⅛ teaspoon pepper
2 teaspoons ground cumin
1 tablespoon chili powder
1 teaspoon garlic powder
¾ cup ripe olives, chopped
½ cup butter
2 tablespoons flour
1½ cups milk
1 16-ounce carton sour cream
2 cups grated Cheddar cheese

Combine water and 2 tablespoons picante sauce in a large shallow dish. Place tortillas in picante sauce mixture and let stand 5 minutes. Drain. Cook ground beef and onion in skillet until brown and then drain. Stir in salt, pepper, cumin, chili powder, garlic powder, olives, and ¼ cup picante sauce. Simmer meat mixture 5 minutes.

Melt butter in a heavy saucepan and add flour, stirring until smooth. Gradually stir in milk. Cook over medium heat, stirring constantly, until thickened and bubbly. Remove from heat and add sour cream. Stir until well blended.

Place half of tortillas in a greased 13x9x2-inch baking dish. Pour half of sour cream sauce over tortillas. Spoon half of the meat mixture evenly over the sauce. Sprinkle half of the cheese over the meat mixture. Repeat layers with remaining ingredients. Bake at 350° for 25 minutes.

May be made ahead and baked just before serving.

Serves 8

PAN BROILED FILET MIGNON

4 4-ounce beef tenderloins, 1-inch thick
3 tablespoons dried green peppercorns
3 tablespoons black peppercorns
½ cup dry vermouth
½ cup beef broth
½ cup brandy

Firmly press peppercorns into filets. In a large skillet over medium high heat, cook filets for 1 minute per side or until browned. Lower heat to medium low and cook 4 minutes on each side or until desired doneness is reached. Remove from pan. Add vermouth and broth to the pan and bring to a boil, scraping the bottom of the pan occasionally. Cook approximately 4 minutes or until the liquid is reduced by half. Add brandy and return to a boil. Reduce again by half. Serve sauce over filets.

Serves 4

Frank Clinesmith

FRENCH DIP SANDWICHES

4 beef bouillon cubes
1 3-4 pound rump roast
1 medium onion
1 tablespoon Worcestershire
Salt
Pepper
2 cans beer
1 can beef consommé
1 loaf French bread

Place bouillon cubes in bottom of a Dutch oven. Place the rump roast on top of the bouillon cubes. Season the roast with salt and pepper. Slice the onion and place on top of seasoned roast. Add Worcestershire, two cans of beer and consommé. Bring to a boil. Reduce heat and simmer covered for 3 to 4 hours. Check occasionally to make sure there is still liquid in the pot. When done, slice beef and serve on toasted French bread or sourdough rolls. Use juice to dip.

Serves 6

KING RANCH BEEF

1½ pounds ground chuck
1   large onion, chopped
1   green pepper, chopped
2   tomatoes, chopped
1   10-ounce can Rotel
    tomatoes
1   package (12) tortillas
1   16-ounce can Ranch
    Style beans
1   pound Velveeta cheese,
    thinly sliced or grated
1   can cream of chicken
    soup
Salt and pepper

Brown meat with onion and pepper. Drain. Add tomatoes, Rotel, salt and pepper to taste. In a 9x13-inch baking dish (use cooking spray), layer ½ each of the tortillas, meat, beans, and cheese. Repeat. Top with the soup. Bake at 350° for 35 to 40 minutes or until bubbly.

May be made ahead of time and refrigerated until ready to bake.

Serves 6 to 8

LASAGNA

1   clove garlic, minced
1   medium onion,
    chopped
½   green pepper, chopped
1½ pounds ground meat
Olive oil
1   can tomato paste
2   tomato paste cans water
1   large can tomatoes
4   teaspoons oregano
2   teaspoons basil
½   teaspoon salt
Pepper
½   teaspoon sugar
¾   package lasagna
    noodles, cooked and
    drained
2   8-ounce cartons sour
    cream
3   8-ounce packages
    mozzarella cheese

Sauté garlic, onion, green pepper and meat in olive oil. Add tomato paste, water, tomatoes, seasonings and sugar. Simmer for 2 to 3 hours. Layer in a large baking dish as follows: noodles, sour cream, sauce and mozzarella. Repeat to make two layers. Bake at 350° for 45 minutes.

This may be made a day ahead and refrigerated until ready to bake.

May also be prepared in two smaller baking dishes, freezing one for later use.

Serves 8 to 10

NACHO CASSEROLE

1 pound ground beef
1 large onion, chopped
1 16-ounce can refried beans
1 4.5-ounce can chopped green chilies
1½ cups grated Cheddar cheese
1½ cups grated Monterey Jack cheese
1 4-ounce can taco sauce
6 green onions, sliced
1 4-ounce can chopped black olives
1 cup guacamole
1 cup sour cream

Brown meat and onion in skillet; drain grease. Spread beans in bottom of 9x13-inch casserole. Spread meat and onion on top of beans. Scatter green chilies and cheeses on top of meat. Pour taco sauce evenly over top layer. Bake at 350° for 30 minutes. Top with green onions and black olives. Let cool 10 minutes then slice and serve in squares. Serve with bowls of guacamole and sour cream.

May also be prepared as a dip and served with tortilla chips for dipping.

Serves 6 to 8

MEAT LOAF

2 pounds ground chuck
1 can tomato soup
1 cup bread crumbs
1 green pepper, chopped, optional
1 onion, chopped
1 egg, slightly beaten
1 tablespoon Worcestershire sauce
1½ teaspoons salt
½ teaspoon pepper

Mix all meat loaf ingredients together and form into a loaf. Place in greased baking dish. Bake at 350° for 1 hour and 15 minutes. During last half hour, top with sauce.

SAUCE

1 can tomato soup
3 tablespoons brown sugar
2 tablespoons mustard
3 tablespoons vinegar
2 teaspoons Worcestershire sauce

Combine all sauce ingredients and pour over meat loaf.

Serves 6

MONTEREY CASSEROLE

2½ pounds ground chuck
1 onion, chopped
1 14.5-ounce can tomatoes, drained
1 10-ounce package frozen chopped spinach, cooked and drained
Salt to taste
Pepper to taste
Tabasco to taste
1 teaspoon Worcestershire
12 flour tortillas
2 4.5-ounce cans chopped green chilies
½ pound sharp Cheddar cheese, grated

In a heavy skillet, brown meat and onion and drain well. Add tomatoes, spinach and seasonings. Simmer uncovered for 5 minutes. Coat a 9x13-inch casserole with cooking spray. Cover bottom of casserole with half of the tortillas. Add the meat mixture, green chilies and cheese. Cover with the other half of the tortillas.

SAUCE

1 can cream of mushroom soup
1 can golden mushroom soup
1 8-ounce carton sour cream
¼ cup milk
¼ teaspoon garlic powder

Mix sauce ingredients and pour over the top of the prepared casserole. Bake at 350° for 45 minutes.

May be made ahead of time and refrigerated or frozen until ready to bake.

Serves 8 to 10

Kathy Daume

POT ROAST

1   2-3 pound pot roast
6   new potatoes, peeled
1   package frozen baby
    carrots
½   package frozen pearl
    onions
1   small jar sliced
    mushrooms, drained
1   package dry onion soup
    mix

Place all ingredients in a crock pot starting with meat and ending with dry soup. Cook on medium or low setting 4 to 5 hours or until meat is done and potatoes are tender.

Serves 4 to 6

SHISH KABOB MARINADE

6   ounces soy sauce
6   ounces salad oil
6   ounces vinegar
2   bunches green onions,
    chopped fine
1   large white onion,
    chopped fine
1   teaspoon ginger
2   tablespoons
    Worcestershire
2   tablespoons brown
    sugar
Dash of garlic powder
5-6 pounds sirloin tips,
    cut in cubes

Combine all of the above in a large flat baking pan, adding meat last. Marinate in refrigerator for several hours, turning occasionally. Put meat on skewers and cook on a hot grill to desired doneness. Brush meat with sauce while cooking.

Try marinating chicken breasts.

Serves 6 to 8

Mom

111

TACO MEAT

1	pound lean ground meat
¼	cup water
3	tablespoons flour
¼	cup chopped onion
1	cup peeled, chopped tomatoes
1	tablespoon chili powder
1	teaspoon cumin
1½	teaspoons salt
1	teaspoon pepper

Brown meat with water until half cooked. Stir in flour and add all other ingredients. Cook over low heat for 10 minutes.

Serves 4

Lucile Finch

SPAGHETTI CASSEROLE

2	pounds ground beef
1	onion, chopped
½	green pepper, chopped
1	32-ounce can tomatoes
1	6-ounce can tomato paste

Garlic salt to taste
Pepper to taste

1½	tablespoons sugar

Pinch of oregano

1	can tomato soup
¼	pound mushrooms, chopped
1	tablespoon butter
1	16-ounce package vermicelli
1	pound grated Cheddar cheese

Sauté mushrooms in butter and set aside. Brown meat, onion and green pepper. Add tomatoes and tomato paste. Fill tomato paste can half full with water and add to mixture. Add seasonings, soup and mushrooms. Simmer for 20 to 30 minutes, stirring occasionally. Break spaghetti into quarters and cook in boiling salted water. Drain and add to meat mixture, mixing well. Remove from heat. Add two-thirds of cheese and stir until melted. Pour into a large casserole and top with remaining cheese. Bake at 325° for 45 minutes or until hot and bubbly.

May be made a day ahead and refrigerated until ready to bake.

Serves 10 to 12

Spaghetti Pie

CRUST

1   8-ounce package spaghetti, cooked and drained
2   tablespoons melted butter
3   tablespoons grated Parmesan cheese
2   eggs, well beaten

Break spaghetti into pieces, cook and drain. Mix spaghetti and remainder of ingredients and press into a deep dish pie plate to form a crust.

FILLING

2   10-ounce packages frozen chopped spinach, cooked and drained
1   clove garlic, minced
1   tablespoon olive oil
¼   cup grated Parmesan cheese
1   egg, well beaten

Mix all filling ingredients and spread over crust.

TOPPING

½   pound ground meat, browned and drained
1   small jar sliced mushrooms, drained
1   14-ounce jar spaghetti sauce

Topping: Add mushrooms and sauce to meat and bring to a boil. Pour over the filling. Top with additional Parmesan or Monterey Jack cheese. Bake at 350° for 30 minutes.

Serves 6 to 8

Mom

Spaghetti Sauce

2	tablespoons olive oil
4	cloves garlic, minced
1	small green pepper, chopped
1	small white onion, chopped
1	pound fresh mushrooms, sliced
1	pound ground round steak
1	pound bulk sausage
1	32-ounce can Italian plum tomatoes, chopped
2	6-ounce cans tomato paste
2	tablespoons parsley flakes
1	teaspoon oregano
1	tablespoon salt
1	teaspoon pepper

Heat oil in a Dutch oven. Add garlic, green pepper, onion and mushrooms and sauté until tender. In a skillet, cook sausage until lightly browned. Drain. Add ground round and sausage to vegetable mixture and cook until meat is no longer pink. Add the remaining ingredients and simmer for 2 hours.

May be made ahead of time or frozen and heated before serving.

Serves 8

Veal Marsala

1½	pounds veal scaloppini
	Salt to taste
	Pepper to taste
4	tablespoons vegetable oil
5	tablespoons butter
¼	cup Marsala wine
3	tablespoons chicken broth
1	tablespoon lemon juice
1	tablespoon chopped parsley

Pound veal with a mallet. Salt and pepper to taste. Dredge veal in flour. In a large skillet, heat half each of the oil and butter. Brown half the veal slices for two minutes on each side. Repeat process using remaining oil, butter and veal. Remove veal to a warm platter. Add wine, broth and lemon juice to skillet. Cook briefly over high heat. Return veal to skillet and cover with sauce. Sprinkle with parsley. Serve on a warm platter with additional parsley for garnish.

Serves 4 to 6

Sue Geren

BAKED CHICKEN BREASTS

4-6 chicken breasts,
    skinless, bone-in
Lemon pepper
1 stick butter, melted
1 package dry onion soup
    mix

Rinse and drain dry each chicken breast. Place chicken in rectangular baking dish (use cooking spray) and season with lemon pepper. Evenly sprinkle the dry soup mix over the chicken. Drizzle butter over soup mix. Bake covered or uncovered for 45 minutes at 350°, basting occasionally.

Serves 4 to 6

CHICKEN CASSEROLE

1 can cream of chicken
    soup
1 can cream of mushroom
    soup
½ cup white wine
½ cup orange juice
1¼ cups raw white rice
6 chicken breasts
1 package dry onion soup
    mix

Mix all liquid ingredients and place in a greased 9x13-inch casserole. Sprinkle rice on top of soup mixture and then place chicken breasts on top of the rice. Sprinkle onion soup over chicken. Cover and bake for 1 hour at 350°.

This casserole may be made the night before and baked just before serving.

Serves 6

Sue McDonnell Grinwis

CERF CHICKEN

6 boneless, skinless chicken breasts
1 stick butter
½ cup chopped green onions
¼ cup chopped parsley
Salt
Pepper
½ cup flour
1½ cups chicken broth
1½ cups half-and-half
½ cup sour cream
Worcestershire sauce

Melt butter in large skillet. Brown chicken lightly. Sprinkle green onions and parsley over the chicken. Cover and simmer about 1 hour. Add salt and pepper after about 45 minutes of cooking. When done, remove chicken and add to the skillet the flour. Cook a few minutes and then add chicken broth, cream, sour cream and a dash of Worcestershire. When sauce thickens, put chicken back in sauce. Heat and serve.

Serves 6

Mom

CHEESY CHICKEN CASSEROLE

6 slices day old bread
4 ounces sharp American cheese, grated
1½ cups cooked chicken, diced
1 can cream of chicken soup
2 eggs, beaten
1 cup milk
2 tablespoons chopped onions
¼ cup bread crumbs
Paprika

Trim crust from bread. Cut in half diagonally. Arrange half of the bread in an 8x8-inch baking dish that has been coated with cooking spray. Sprinkle cheese over the bread. Add chicken and remaining bread. In a separate bowl, combine eggs and soup and mix well. Add onions and milk to soup. Pour over casserole. Cover and refrigerate 6 to 24 hours. Before baking, sprinkle with bread crumbs and paprika. Bake at 325° for one hour. Let stand 10 minutes before serving.

Serves 6

Judy Hawley

COUNTRYSIDE CHICKEN BAKE

1 cup uncooked long-grain rice
¾ cup chopped onion
2 tablespoons butter or margarine, melted
2 teaspoons dried parsley flakes
¼ teaspoon salt
⅛ teaspoon pepper
6 chicken breast halves
1 can cream of mushroom soup
⅔ cup mayonnaise
¼ cup milk
Paprika

Cook rice according to package directions. Combine rice with onion, butter, parsley, salt and pepper. Mix well. Spoon into a lightly greased 13x9x2-inch baking dish; top with chicken breasts. In a mixing bowl, combine soup, mayonnaise and milk; spoon mixture over the chicken breasts. Bake, uncovered at 350° for 1 hour. Sprinkle with paprika if desired.

Serves 6

CHICKEN DIJON

4 chicken breast halves
3 tablespoons butter
2 tablespoons all purpose flour
1 cup chicken broth
½ cup half-and-half
2 tablespoons Dijon style mustard

In a large skillet, sauté chicken in butter until well browned. Remove chicken from the pan. Add flour to the skillet and stir until smooth. Add broth and half-and-half, stirring constantly to avoid lumps; add mustard and mix well. Return chicken to pan and simmer in sauce for 30 minutes. Serve over rice or noodles.

Serves 3 to 4

Sue Geren

117

DOUGLASS RANCH CHICKEN

6   boneless, skinless, chicken breasts, cooked and cubed
1   tablespoon butter or margarine
1   medium onion, diced
1   clove garlic, chopped
2   cans cream of mushroom soup
1   can cream of chicken soup
1½ cans Rotel tomatoes
2   cups grated Cheddar cheese
1   dozen corn tortillas, broken into pieces
1   teaspoon lemon pepper

Sauté onion and garlic in butter until tender. Set aside. In a medium mixing bowl, combine soups, Rotel and sautéed vegetables. Coat a 9x13-inch casserole with cooking spray. Place half of the tortillas on the bottom of the casserole. Follow with half the chicken. Pour half the soup mixture over chicken and then sprinkle half of the cheese over the soup mixture. Repeat the process for the second layer, sprinkling the soup layer with lemon pepper. Bake at 350° for 45 minutes.

May be made ahead and refrigerated or frozen until ready to bake.

Serves 6 to 8

Janie Douglass

FRIDAY NIGHT ROASTED CHICKEN

1   whole chicken
     (3-4 pounds)
1   teaspoon paprika
1   teaspoon onion powder
1   teaspoon garlic powder
1   teaspoon salt
4   teaspoons vegetable oil
½   teaspoon pepper

In a small bowl mix all ingredients except the chicken. Place the chicken in roasting pan and rub the seasoning mixture on the chicken until well coated. Bake uncovered at 325° for 1½ hours or until the chicken is done and the skin is crispy. Baste occasionally while cooking.

Kathleen Livingston

BASTED GRILLED CHICKEN

6   chicken breasts,
     bone-in
2   tablespoons butter,
     melted
2   tablespoons
     mayonnaise
1   teaspoon lemon juice
2   tablespoons white wine
¼   teaspoon thyme
¼   teaspoon garlic powder
¼   teaspoon salt
¼   teaspoon basil
¼   teaspoon parsley
Pepper to taste
1   teaspoon hot sweet
     mustard
1   tablespoon brown sugar

Mix all ingredients with a wire whisk and baste chicken while grilling or broiling. Watch chicken carefully to avoid burning. Paint chicken liberally with sauce before serving.

Serves 4 to 6

Carolyn B. Wallace

119

Honey Chicken

6 chicken breasts, boneless, skinless
⅓ cup butter
⅔ cup honey
¼ cup prepared mustard
4 teaspoons curry powder

Melt butter and add honey, mustard and curry powder. Mix well. Roll chicken in mixture and place in a well-greased baking dish. Bake for 45 minutes at 375°. Turn and baste often. Cover for last 15 minutes.

Serves 4 to 6

Imperial Chicken

6 chicken breasts, boneless, skinless
2 cups bread crumbs
¾ cup Parmesan cheese, grated
¼ cup chopped parsley
¼ teaspoon garlic salt
2 teaspoons salt
⅛ teaspoon pepper
1 cup butter or margarine, melted

Combine bread crumbs, Parmesan cheese, parsley, salts and pepper. Dip each piece of chicken into melted butter and then into crumb mixture. Arrange in shallow roasting pan (use cooking spray). Pour remaining butter over chicken and bake at 350° for 30 to 45 minutes or until brown.

Serves 4 to 6

Marti Clinesmith

One Dish Chicken

½ cup water
½ can cream of mushroom soup
½ package dried onion soup
¼ cup dry sherry
⅔ cup raw rice
6 chicken breasts

Stir together all ingredients except chicken. Place in a greased 9x13-inch baking dish. Place chicken on top. Season with salt and pepper. Cover and bake at 350°. Uncover and bake an additional 15 minutes.

Serves 4 to 6

OVERNIGHT CHICKEN

3 whole boneless, skinless chicken breasts, halved
½ cup honey
½ cup Dijon mustard
1 tablespoon curry powder
2 tablespoons soy sauce

Place chicken, skin side down, in a baking dish that has been coated with cooking spray. Mix honey, mustard, curry and soy sauce. Pour over chicken and refrigerate for 6 hours or overnight, covered. Turn chicken over, cover pan with aluminum foil and bake one hour at 350°. Baste with sauce and continue baking, uncovered, for 15 minutes.

Serves 4 to 6

POPPY SEED CHICKEN

8 boneless, skinless chicken breasts
2 cans cream of chicken soup
1 16-ounce carton sour cream
1-2 tablespoons poppy seeds
Buttered cracker crumbs

Boil chicken breasts until tender. Cool and cube. Mix soup, sour cream and poppy seeds. Add cubed chicken. Pour mixture into baking dish (use cooking spray.) Cover with cracker crumbs. Bake for 1 hour at 325° - covered for the first 30 minutes. Serve over white rice.

May be made the night before. Just add the cracker crumbs before baking. Also note, this recipe is easily halved.

Serves 8

Anne Harrison

CHICKEN & RICE

1 3 to 4 pound whole chicken
1½ cups white rice
3 cups of liquid (broth and cream)
Seasoning to taste

Clean chicken and put in a 4-quart deep baking dish that has been coated with cooking spray. Add about a ½ cup of water and bake covered at 325° for 1 to 1½ hours. Remove chicken, add rice, and 3 cups of liquid. This can be a combination of broth from baking dish and cream. Continue baking, uncovered, for approximately 40 minutes or until rice is cooked.

Serves 4 to 6

Marti Clinesmith

CHICKEN SHISH KABOB

MARINADE

⅔ cup soy sauce
¼ cup vegetable oil
6 cloves garlic, minced
2 teaspoons MSG, optional
2 teaspoons ground ginger
2 teaspoons dry mustard
2 tablespoons molasses

Mix all marinade ingredients in a glass bowl and leave at room temperature for 8 to 24 hours.

KABOBS

2 pounds chicken breasts, skinned, boned and cut into 1-inch cubes
1 pound fresh mushroom caps
4 onions, quartered
2 bell peppers, cut into chunks
Pineapple chunks, optional

Marinate chicken cubes for 4 to 6 hours - no longer. Arrange chicken and vegetables on skewers and grill on preheated rack for 5 minutes on each side.

Serves 4 to 6

Sue Geren

SIMPLE CHICKEN

6-8 boneless, skinless
chicken breasts
4 tablespoons butter or
margarine
Garlic salt
Pepper
1 can cream of mushroom
soup or cream of onion
1 8-ounce carton sour
cream

Melt butter in a skillet and lightly sauté chicken breasts. Keep liquid in the skillet. Remove chicken breasts and place in rectangular (use cooking spray) baking dish. Add soup and sour cream to skillet and heat. Drizzle sauce over chicken and bake at 350° for 30 to 45 minutes. Serve with rice or noodles. Use the sauce as a gravy.

This may be put together ahead of time and refrigerated until ready to bake.

Serves 6 to 8

SIMPLE CHICKEN #2

4 boneless, skinless
chicken breasts
⅓ cup nonfat plain yogurt
⅓ cup apricot or raspberry
all-fruit preserves
1 tablespoon Dijon-style
mustard

Rinse chicken and pat dry with a paper towel. Place in a single layer in a shallow baking dish that has been coated with cooking spray. In a separate bowl, combine remaining ingredients. Spread over chicken breasts. Bake uncovered for 45 minutes at 350°.

Serves 4

CHICKEN SPAGHETTI

4 boneless, skinless
  chicken breasts
2 carrots, chopped
1 medium onion,
  chopped
Salt, pepper, and garlic
  powder to taste
1 can cream of chicken
  soup
1 can cream of mushroom
  soup
1 can Cheddar cheese
  soup
1 8-ounce package
  spaghetti

Cook chicken breasts in water with carrots, onions, salt, pepper and garlic powder. Strain and reserve stock. Cube chicken. Combine soups and add chicken. Cook spaghetti in reserved stock and drain. Combine chicken mixture with spaghetti and bake covered for 1 hour at 350°.

Serves 4 to 6

Marti Clinesmith

CHICKEN SPAGHETTI #2

8 chicken breasts,
  skinless, bone-in
½ green pepper, chopped
1 cup onion, chopped
1 can mushrooms, drained
  and chopped
½ package vermicelli,
  broken
½ can diced tomatoes with
  juice
½ can diced Rotel tomatoes
1 can cream of mushroom
  soup
1 pound Velveeta cheese,
  grated
Salt
Pepper
Worcestershire sauce
Garlic salt

Cook chicken breasts in seasoned water until done. Remove chicken and dice. Cook vermicelli, green pepper and onion in chicken broth. Drain and add vermicelli and chicken with remaining ingredients. Place in greased casserole and bake at 350° until well heated.

Serves 6

Gail Clark

SPICY CHICKEN SPAGHETTI

2	cups butter
3	cloves garlic, minced
1	teaspoon coarse ground pepper
½	teaspoon salt
4	tablespoons chili powder
4	tablespoons cumin seed
1	medium onion, chopped
1	pound mushrooms, sliced
2	pounds chicken breasts, cooked and diced
¾	pound spaghetti
1	small can chopped black olives

Green onion, chopped
Parmesan cheese, grated

In a large skillet, melt butter. Add garlic and spices, and cook for a few minutes. Sauté onion and mushrooms in the mixture. Add cooked chicken to mushroom sauce. Cook spaghetti in chicken broth until just done. Rinse and drain. Place spaghetti in a greased 9x12-inch dish. Pour sauce and olives over spaghetti and toss well. Bake at 350° for 20 minutes. Top each serving with green onion and Parmesan cheese.

Serves 8

ZIPLOC CHICKEN

4	skinless chicken breasts
1	small onion, sliced
2	garlic cloves, peeled and minced
6	tablespoons lime juice (2 or 3 limes)
1	tablespoon olive oil
¼	teaspoon salt

Place all ingredients in a large ziploc bag and marinate overnight or at least 8 hours. Grill chicken. Sauté onions and serve with the chicken.

Serves 4

Marti Clinesmith

125

Easy Chicken Tetrazzini

6   boneless, skinless
    chicken breasts
½   stick butter
1   4.5-ounce jar sliced
    mushrooms, drained
1   tablespoon parsley
    flakes
2   cans cream of chicken
    soup
½   pint sour cream
Garlic salt
Pepper
1   12-ounce package
    vermicelli
Parmesan cheese

Boil chicken breasts in seasoned water until tender. Cool and cut into bite size pieces. Melt butter in a large skillet and add mushrooms. Sauté 10 minutes. Add parsley flakes and chicken. Cover and let sit for 10 minutes. Add the cream of chicken soup and sour cream. Break the vermicelli into bite size pieces and cook in the chicken stock. Drain and cool. Combine chicken mixture with the vermicelli and place in a buttered casserole. Sprinkle with cheese and bake uncovered at 300° until hot.

May be made ahead and refrigerated before baking.

Serves 8 to 10

Cornish Game Hens

6   Cornish Game Hens
Garlic salt
Pepper
1   cup margarine, divided
    use
½   cup beef consommé
½   cup red wine
6   strips bacon

Season hens to taste with garlic salt and pepper. Brown hens well in ½ cup margarine. Remove from skillet and place in a shallow baking dish. Secure the legs with bacon. Combine ½ cup of margarine (melted), consommé and red wine and pour over the hens. Bake at 350° for 30 minutes and continue basting. Turn heat to 325° for 40 minutes. If the hens get too brown, simply cover with foil.

Serves 6

JAKE'S BIRDS

Dove or Quail -
    as many as you like
    or have on hand
Meat tenderizer
2 sticks butter
Lemon pepper

Sprinkle tenderizer on each bird individually, 20 to 30 minutes before broiling. Melt butter and add lemon pepper to taste. Do not add salt. Baste birds. For dove, broil 4 to 5 minutes on breast side. Turn and continue broiling for another 3 minutes. Quail will take several minutes more per side. Baste several times while cooking. Serve with remaining butter sauce if desired.

Mil Shapira

HAM LOAF

⅔ pound cured ham, ground
1⅓ pounds fresh pork, ground
1 cup fine bread crumbs
¼ teaspoon pepper
2 eggs, beaten
1 cup milk
⅓ cup brown sugar
1 tablespoon dry mustard
¼ cup vinegar

Combine meats, bread crumbs, pepper, eggs and milk. Mix thoroughly and form into a loaf. Place in a greased loaf pan. Mix sugar, mustard and vinegar and pour over the meat. Bake for 1 hour at 350°. Serve with horseradish sauce.

HORSERADISH SAUCE
½ cup whipping cream
3 tablespoons horseradish, drained
½ teaspoon salt

Sauce: Whip cream and add horseradish and salt. Refrigerate until ready to serve.

Serves 6 to 8

HONEY MUSTARD PORK CHOPS

6 pork chops (not too thin)
Salt and pepper to taste
1 tablespoon vegetable oil
⅓ cup orange juice
1½ tablespoons Dijon mustard
1 tablespoon honey
2 teaspoons cornstarch

Season and brown pork chops in oil. Combine orange juice, mustard, honey and cornstarch and mix well. Pour over pork chops, cover and continue cooking over low heat about 30 minutes.

Serves 4 to 6

ONION GLAZED PORK CHOPS

2 tablespoons cornstarch
½ cup water
1 tablespoon margarine
6 pork chops
1 can French onion soup
2 tablespoons brown sugar, firmly packed

Stir together cornstarch and water and completely dissolve. In a large skillet, melt margarine and add pork chops. Season with salt and pepper. Brown on both sides. Remove chops from skillet. Add soup and sugar to pan and bring to a boil. Return chops to pan. Cover and cook over low heat until chops are cooked, stirring occasionally. Remove chops and add cornstarch mixture and heat until thickened. Serve over pork chops.

Serves 4 to 6

PORK CHOPS AND RICE

6   pork chops
Salt and pepper to taste
1   stick plus 1 tablespoon butter
1   can beef consommé
1   can French onion soup
1   cup raw rice
1   4.5-ounce jar sliced mushrooms, drained, optional

Brown pork chops in 1 tablespoon butter. Season while browning. In a 12x7½ x2-inch baking dish (use cooking spray) melt 1 stick of butter.

Add soups, rice and mushrooms. Place browned pork chops on top of rice mixture and bake uncovered at 350° for 45 minutes or until rice is cooked.

May be assembled the night before and refrigerated until time to bake.

Serves 4 to 6

DIJON PORK TENDERS

2   pork tenderloins
5   tablespoons Dijon mustard
3   teaspoons sage

Combine mustard and sage and mix well. Spread mixture on tenderloins. Bake at 350° for 30 minutes or until desired doneness is achieved.

MARINATED PORK TENDERLOIN

2   pounds pork tenderloin
½   teaspoon ground ginger
½   medium onion, minced
2   cloves garlic, minced
1   teaspoon crushed basil leaves
1½   teaspoons parsley
3   tablespoons soy sauce
2   tablespoons salad oil

Combine all ingredients except pork in food processor. Blend until well mixed. Place pork tenderloin in a plastic bag and cover with marinade. Let marinate in refrigerator for anywhere from 1 hour to overnight. Grill over hot coals.

MARINATED PORK TENDERLOIN #2

¼ **cup soy sauce**
2 **tablespoons dry red wine**
1 **tablespoon honey**
1 **tablespoon brown sugar**
1 **clove garlic, minced**
½ **teaspoon cinnamon**
1 **green onion, chopped**
2 **lean pork tenderloins**

Mix first seven ingredients together and pour into a large plastic bag or airtight container. Add tenderloins and marinate for 2 to 24 hours. Remove tenderloins bake at 375° for 40 minutes. Baste with marinade every 15 minutes. May be cooked on the grill for same amount of time. Again, baste every 15 minutes.

BARBECUED SPARE RIBS

3-4 **pounds spare ribs**
2 **onions, sliced**
2 **teaspoons vinegar**
2 **teaspoons Worcestershire**
1 **teaspoon salt**
1 **teaspoon paprika**
½ **teaspoon red pepper**
½ **teaspoon black pepper**
1 **teaspoon chili powder**
¾ **cup ketchup**
¾ **cup water**

Cut spare ribs into individual pieces. Place in roaster and sprinkle with salt and pepper. Cover with onions. Combine remaining ingredients and pour over meat. Cover and bake at 350° about 1½ hours. Baste occasionally, turning spare ribs once or twice. Remove cover last 15 minutes to brown.

Serves 4 to 6

SHRIMP BREAD

1	pound butter, softened
½	cup chopped fresh parsley
¼	cup finely chopped green onions
1½	tablespoons finely minced garlic (or to taste)
1	tablespoon white wine
1½	teaspoons salt
1	teaspoon fresh ground black pepper
¼	cup finely chopped almonds or pine nuts
1	large loaf French Bread
2	pounds raw shrimp
¼	cup white wine

Preheat oven to 400°. Combine butter, parsley, onions, garlic, wine, salt, pepper and nuts to make a spread. Slice top ⅓ off loaf of bread and set aside. Hollow out bottom. Grind removed bread to crumbs. Shell and define shrimp and chop into chunks. In the following order layer in the hollowed loaf: ½ of the seasoned butter, shrimp, 1 tablespoon white wine sprinkled over shrimp, remaining seasoned butter, and finally the bread crumbs. Sprinkle loaf with ¼ cup white wine. Place loaf on cookie sheet and bake uncovered for 35 minutes. Cover bread with bread lid for last 10 minutes of baking. Cut into slices to serve.

Serve with a green salad for a complete and filling meal.

Serves 8

Sue Geren

SHRIMP AND RICE

3	sticks butter
1	bunch green onions, chopped
1	clove fresh garlic, minced
¼	cup white wine
1	tablespoon crushed pepper
1	lemon, juiced
1	box Near East rice pilaf
2	pounds fresh raw shrimp

Melt butter in large saucepan or Dutch oven. Add onions, garlic and pepper and sauté. When ready to serve, add wine, lemon and shrimp. Cook over medium heat until shrimp is pink. Serve over rice - prepared as directed on the box.

Serves 6

Janice Gustafson

131

BUNNY'S SHRIMP

2 pounds large raw shrimp
2 sticks butter
1 cup oil
2 tablespoons garlic puree or 5 cloves, minced
2 teaspoons rosemary
½ teaspoon basil
½ teaspoon oregano
½ teaspoon salt
½ teaspoon red pepper
1 teaspoon paprika
¾ tablespoon lemon juice
1 teaspoon parsley flakes
1 tablespoon Worcestershire sauce

In a large saucepan or Dutch oven, mix all ingredients except shrimp. Simmer 8 minutes and cool. Add shrimp and cook for 8 to 10 minutes or until shrimp is done. Serve in large bowls with French bread for dunking.

Serves 4 to 6

Daisy Welsh

SHRIMP/CRAWFISH CARDINALE

3 green onions, white only, chopped
6 tablespoons butter
2 tablespoons flour
1 cup light cream
¼ cup ketchup
¾ teaspoon salt
¼ teaspoon white pepper
½ teaspoon Tabasco sauce
2 teaspoons lemon juice
1 ounce brandy
1 pound cooked, peeled shrimp or crawfish tails

Sauté green onions in 4 tablespoons butter for 5 minutes. In a separate saucepan, melt 2 tablespoons butter. Add flour, cream and ketchup. Cook until thickened. Add salt, pepper, Tabasco and lemon juice. Flame brandy and slowly stir into sauce. Add sautéed onions and seafood. Cook on low setting until heated. Serve over rice or angel hair pasta.

Serves 6

Sandra Cason

BBQ SHRIMP AND GRITS

GRITS

1 cup heavy cream
1 stick butter
1 quart water
2 cups quick-cooking hominy grits
Salt and white pepper to taste

Heat cream and water to boil. Add butter, salt and pepper. Slowly add grits and reduce heat. Cook 20 minutes, being careful not to scorch mixture.

BBQ SAUCE

¼ pound bacon, cooked and crumbled
½ cup red onions, chopped finely
½ cup red bell peppers, chopped finely
½ cup green peppers, chopped finely
3½ cups ketchup
½ cup brown sugar
3-4 tablespoons Southern Comfort, optional
Salt and pepper to taste

Sauce: Sauté onions and peppers in bacon drippings. Return bacon to pan and then flame with Southern Comfort, if desired. Add ketchup, sugar and salt and pepper. Simmer for 10 minutes and cool.

TOPPING

2 pounds shrimp, peeled and deveined
¼ pound bacon, cooked and crumbled
½ cup green onions, sliced
1 cup Cheddar cheese, grated

Topping: Sauté or poach shrimp in 1 tablespoon butter. Place in BBQ Sauce and simmer for 1 minute. Pour grits into individual bowls. Top with BBQ Shrimp, remaining crumbled bacon, green onions and grated cheese.

BBQ Sauce will last refrigerated for several weeks.

Serves 6

Anne DeuPree Duke

COMPANY SHRIMP CASSEROLE

2-3 pounds cooked, peeled shrimp
1 cup rice, cooked
1 cup sharp Cheddar cheese, grated
1 can cream of mushroom soup
½ cup chopped green pepper
½ cup chopped onion
1 stick butter
4 lemons, thinly sliced
Salt
Pepper

Mix first four ingredients. Sauté green pepper and onion in butter and add to shrimp mixture. Season to taste with salt and pepper. Put in a long, flat casserole (use cooking spray) and completely cover with lemon slices. Bake covered for 20 minutes at 375°.

Serves 6

Mom

SHRIMP CURRY

½ cup chopped onion
½ cup chopped green pepper
¼ cup butter
1 tablespoon flour
2 teaspoons curry powder
½ teaspoon salt
Dash of ginger
1 16-ounce carton sour cream
24 ounces shrimp, cooked and peeled

Sauté onion and green pepper in butter until tender. Stir in flour, curry powder, salt, and ginger. Add sour cream and mix thoroughly. Add shrimp and cook over low heat. Do not allow to boil. Serve over rice.

Serves 4

Lucile Finch

ISLAND SHRIMP

1	cup croutons
1	teaspoon curry powder
½	teaspoon onion powder
½	teaspoon pepper, use cayenne if you like it spicy
2	eggs
2	tablespoons water
½	stick of butter, melted
30	large shrimp, peeled and deveined

In a blender, combine croutons, curry powder, onion powder and pepper. Mix until just blended and transfer to a shallow bowl. In a separate bowl, slightly beat eggs with water. Dip shrimp in egg mixture, then roll in crumbs. Place on a well-greased cookie sheet. Drizzle butter over shrimp. Bake at 350° for 6 minutes.

May be served as an appetizer.

Serve 4

Kathy Daume

ORIENTAL BARBECUED SHRIMP

2	pounds raw shrimp, peeled and deveined
½	teaspoon salt
Pepper	
1	tablespoon honey
2	tablespoons soy sauce
1	tablespoon dry sherry
3	tablespoons vegetable oil
2	tablespoons minced scallions

Place shrimp in a flat baking dish that has been coated with cooking spray. Blend together salt, pepper, honey, soy sauce and sherry. Add oil and mix thoroughly. Pour over shrimp and let marinate about 15 minutes. Bake at 375° for 10 minutes. Do not overcook. Shrimp is done when it turns pink. Sprinkle with scallions before serving.

Serves 6

SAUCY SHRIMP

5 pounds raw shrimp
1 pound butter or margarine
5 cloves garlic, minced
3 bay leaves
½ teaspoon basil
Salt to taste
5 heaping tablespoons coarsely ground black pepper
5 lemons, juiced

Preheat oven to 375°. Melt butter in a large open pan. Add all remaining ingredients. Stir to coat shrimp. Bake uncovered for 40 to 50 minutes. Remove from oven and allow to cool slightly.

Serve with tossed salad and plenty of French bread for dipping. Spread newspaper over table for easy clean-up.

Serves 8

Sue Geren

CRAB CAKES

2 pounds lump crab meat
3 eggs
1 tablespoon Dijon mustard
3 tablespoons heavy cream
1 teaspoon Worcestershire sauce
2 teaspoons Old Bay Seasonings
⅛ teaspoon cayenne pepper
3 tablespoons minced green onions
2 tablespoons minced parsley
½ cup mayonnaise
3 tablespoons finely crushed soda crackers
1 cup fine dry bread crumbs
1 stick butter
4 tablespoons cooking oil

Remove any shell and cartilage from crab meat. In a bowl, whisk the eggs and then add cream, mustard, Worcestershire sauce, Old Bay Seasoning and cayenne. Mix well. Add green onions, parsley and mayonnaise and mix until all is well blended. Gently fold in crab meat and crackers. Form the mixture into 8 cakes and lightly coat each with bread crumbs. Cover and chill for approximately 1 hour. Sauté cakes in butter and oil for 3 to 4 minutes in a heavy skillet until golden brown.

Serves 8

DEVILED CRAB

3 tablespoons flour
3 tablespoons butter
½ teaspoon salt
⅛ teaspoon paprika
½ small onion, grated
Pepper
¼ teaspoon A-1 sauce
1 cup milk
1 cup chicken stock or broth
1 can crab meat, drained and checked for shell
2 hard boiled eggs, sliced
1 4.5-ounce jar sliced mushrooms, drained
1 tablespoon capers
1 cup cracker crumbs
2 eggs, stiffly beaten
1 cup grated Parmesan cheese

Melt butter and add flour to make a roux. Add milk and chicken broth slowly and continue to stir. As sauce begins to thicken, add salt, paprika, pepper, A-1 sauce, and onion. When desired thickness is reached, add crab meat, eggs, mushrooms, capers and cracker crumbs. Mix together and then add eggs. Put in ramekins or greased baking dish. Cover with cracker crumbs, Parmesan cheese and paprika. Bake for 30 minutes at 300°.

Serves 6

Mom

ALMOND CRUSTED SOLE

2 pounds fillet of sole
Salt and pepper
1 cup sour cream
2 tablespoons lemon juice
2 tablespoons Worcestershire sauce
1 teaspoon dill weed
1 teaspoon onion powder
1 cup finely chopped blanched almonds
2 tablespoons butter
2 tablespoons oil

Sprinkle fish lightly with salt and pepper. Mix sour cream with lemon juice, Worcestershire, dill and onion powder. Coat fish fillets on both sides with this mixture. Press chopped nuts into fish. In a large skillet, heat oil and butter over medium heat. Sauté fish until golden brown on both sides.

Serves 6

Baked Fish

4   fish fillets (grouper,
    orange roughy, etc.)
1   cup milk
2   lemons, sliced
½   cup butter, melted
Salt
Pepper

Soak fish fillets in milk for 30 minutes. Drain fish and place in a greased baking dish. Place lemon slices on each fillet. Drizzle melted butter over fish and then season to taste. Bake at 350° for about 15 minutes or until fish flakes easily with a fork.

Serves 4

Broiled Fish

2   pounds fish fillets
2   tablespoons lemon
    juice
½   cup grated Parmesan
    cheese
¼   cup margarine, softened
3   tablespoons
    mayonnaise
3   tablespoons chopped
    green onion
¼   teaspoon salt
Tabasco sauce

Place fillets in a single layer on a well-greased baking platter. Brush with lemon juice. Combine remaining ingredients. Broil fillets about 4 inches from heat for 4 to 6 minutes or until fish flakes easily. Remove from heat and spread with mayonnaise mixture. Broil 2 to 3 minutes more or until lightly browned.

Serves 6

GRILLED FISH

4-6 boneless fish fillets
    (grouper, orange
    roughy, etc.)
Lemon slices
Squeeze margarine
Seasoning to taste
Aluminum foil

Arrange each fillet on an individual piece of aluminum foil that has been coated with cooking spray. Place two lemon slices on each, squeeze margarine over lemon and season to taste. Seal the aluminum foil tightly and place on hot grill. Cook about five minutes, turn and cook another five minutes.

Serves 4 to 6

FISH PARMESAN

6 fish fillets
1 cup seasoned bread
   crumbs, finely crushed
¾ cup grated Parmesan
   cheese
¼ cup chopped parsley
1 teaspoon paprika
½ teaspoon oregano
¼ teaspoon basil
2 teaspoons salt
½ teaspoon pepper
¼ cup melted butter

Pat fish dry. Combine crumbs, cheese and seasonings; mix well. Dip fish in melted butter and roll in crumb mixture. Arrange in well-greased 13x9x2-inch baking dish. Bake at 375° for about 25 minutes.

Serves 4 to 6

Desserts

APPLE BUTTERMILK CAKE

1 box spice cake mix
1 small box instant
vanilla pudding
¾ cup oil
1 cup buttermilk
4 eggs
2 large apples, peeled
and chopped
1 cup chopped pecans,
optional
Powdered sugar

Combine cake mix and pudding. Add oil, buttermilk and eggs and mix well. Stir in apples and pecans. Bake in a well-greased bundt pan at 350° for 50 minutes. When cake has cooled, sprinkle with powdered sugar or serve with warm buttermilk sauce.

BUTTERMILK SAUCE

1 cup sugar
½ cup butter
½ cup buttermilk
1 tablespoon light corn
syrup
2 teaspoons vanilla
½ teaspoon baking soda

Combine all sauce ingredients in a saucepan. Boil over medium heat, stirring constantly.

This cake is a great dessert but also may be served as a coffee cake.

Makes about 2 cups

Kathy Daume

APRICOT NECTAR CAKE

1 package Gladiola
Pound cake mix
1 package lemon Jell-O
4 eggs
½ cup oil
1 teaspoon lemon extract
¾ cup apricot nectar

Blend all ingredients and bake in a well-greased tube pan at 350° for 1 hour.

LEMON GLAZE

1 cup powdered sugar
Juice of one lemon

Mix powdered sugar and lemon juice and drizzle over the hot cake.

Mom

BAILEY'S CHOCOLATE CHIP CHEESECAKE

CRUST

2 cups graham cracker crumbs
¼ cup sugar
6 tablespoons butter, melted

FILLING

36 ounces cream cheese, at room temperature
1⅔ cups sugar
5 eggs, at room temperature
1 cup Bailey's Irish Cream
1 tablespoon vanilla
1 cup semisweet chocolate chips

COFFEE CREAM

1 cup whipping cream
2 tablespoons sugar
1 teaspoon instant coffee powder

Preheat oven to 325°. Spray a 9-inch springform pan or 9x13-inch Pyrex dish with cooking spray. Mix crust ingredients and press in pan. Bake 7 minutes.

To prepare filling, cream sugar and cream cheese. Add eggs, one at a time, blending well with each addition. Add Bailey's and vanilla. Sprinkle half of the chocolate chips on crust. Pour filling over chips and then sprinkle the remaining half of chocolate chips. Bake 1 hour 20 minutes if using a springform pan, less for 9x13-inch pan. Cool.

Whip all coffee cream ingredients in a chilled bowl, with chilled mixer. Spread over cooled cake.

Kathy Daume

143

BANANA CAKE

2	cups sugar
1½	cups salad oil
3	eggs
4	ripe bananas
3	cups flour
1	teaspoon cinnamon
1	teaspoon nutmeg
½	teaspoon salt
2	teaspoons baking soda
1	cup pecans, chopped, optional

Mix sugar and oil until well blended. Add eggs one at a time, beating between each addition. Break up bananas in chunks and add to batter. Sift flour. Add cinnamon, nutmeg, salt, soda and sift again. Add slowly to the batter and continue beating. Fold in pecans. Grease and flour a bundt pan. Bake for 1 hour at 350°. Let cool for 30 minutes before removing from pan. Frost cake when completely cooled.

ICING

1	stick butter, softened
1	8-ounce package cream cheese, softened
1	box powdered sugar
1	teaspoon vanilla

To make icing, cream butter and cream cheese. Add powdered sugar and vanilla and blend thoroughly.

BLUEBERRY STREUSEL

6	cups fresh blueberries
3	tablespoons fresh lemon juice
⅔	cup firmly packed brown sugar
½	cup flour
¼	teaspoon salt
¼	teaspoon nutmeg
¼	cup butter

Whipped cream, whipped

Mix blueberries with lemon juice and pour into a buttered 9-inch square baking dish. In a separate bowl, mix sugar with flour, salt and nutmeg. Cut in butter coarsely. Rub between fingers until well blended. Sprinkle mixture evenly over berries. Bake for 20 minutes at 375°. Serve warm with whipped cream.

Serves 6 to 8

BUTTERSCOTCH PUDDING CAKE

1 box yellow cake mix
2 3-ounce packages butterscotch instant pudding mix
3 eggs
2 tablespoons mayonnaise
1½ cups water

Combine all ingredients in a large mixing bowl and beat with an electric mixer until smooth. Pour into a well-greased 9x13-inch baking pan. Bake at 350° for 35 minutes or until cake tests done. Allow cake to cool before frosting.

BROWN SUGAR ICING

1 3-ounce package cream cheese, softened
1 cup firmly packed brown sugar
½ teaspoon vanilla
2 4-ounce containers frozen whipped topping, thawed

Icing: In a bowl, mix cream cheese, brown sugar and vanilla until fluffy. Fold in frozen whipped topping. Spread over cooled cake.

MISSISSIPPI MUD CAKE

4 eggs
2 cups sugar
2 sticks butter or margarine
⅓ cup cocoa
1½ cups flour
1 teaspoon baking powder
1½ cups finely chopped pecans, optional
1 teaspoon vanilla
1 jar marshmallow cream

Blend the eggs, sugar and melted butter until well mixed. Add flour, baking powder and pecans. Mix well and add vanilla. Pour the mixture into a well-greased and floured 9x13-inch pan. Bake at 350° for 30 minutes. While the mixture is still hot, cover with marshmallow cream.

CHOCOLATE ICING

1 stick melted margarine
6 teaspoons milk
⅓ cup cocoa
1 box powdered sugar

Mix melted margarine, milk, cocoa, and powdered sugar until smooth and pour over the marshmallow cream.

CARROT CAKE

2 cups sugar
1½ cups vegetable oil
4 eggs
2 cups flour
2 teaspoons baking soda
1 teaspoon salt
2 teaspoons cinnamon
2 teaspoons vanilla
3 cups finely grated carrots

Cream sugar and oil with electric beaters. Add eggs one at a time, beating well after each addition. Sift together dry ingredients. Add carrots and flour mixture. Add vanilla a mix well. Bake in well-greased 8 or 9-inch layer pans at 350° for 30 to 40 minutes. Allow to cool and then ice.

CREAM CHEESE FROSTING

1 8-ounce package cream cheese, softened
¼ pound margarine, softened
1 box powdered sugar
1 teaspoon vanilla
1 cup chopped pecans, optional

Icing: Cream together cream cheese and margarine. Add remaining ingredients and mix well.

If desired, this recipe makes about 60 cupcakes. Bake at same temperature for about 20 minutes.

Mom

CHOCOLATE PUDDIN' CAKE

1 cup flour
1 stick butter
1 cup finely chopped pecans
1 cup powdered sugar
1 8-ounce package cream cheese, softened
1 large container frozen dairy topping, divided use
1 package instant chocolate pudding
1 package instant vanilla pudding
2 cups milk
Shaved chocolate, optional

Blend flour, softened butter and nuts. Spread on the bottom of a large baking dish (use cooking spray). Bake at 350° for 20 minutes. Cool. With a mixer, combine cream cheese and sugar. Add 1 cup frozen dairy topping. Spread this over cooled crust. Combine puddings with milk and beat until of a spreading consistency. Spread on top of cream cheese mixture. Top with remainder of frozen dairy topping. May finish with shaved chocolate if desired.

Vers

CHOCOLATE CAKE

2	cups sugar
1	cup shortening
2	eggs
1	cup buttermilk
2¼	cups flour
¼	cup cocoa
½	teaspoon salt
2	teaspoons baking soda
1	cup boiling coffee
1	teaspoon vanilla
1	small bottle red food coloring

In a large bowl, cream shortening and sugar with electric beaters. Add eggs. Sift together flour, cocoa, and salt. Alternately add buttermilk and flour mixture to creamed mixture. When well blended, add baking soda, coffee, vanilla, and food coloring. Mix well and bake in a well-greased sheet pan or large loaf pan at 350° for 45 minutes or until center tests clean with a cake tester or toothpick. Ice while cake is still hot.

CHOCOLATE COCOA ICING

1	stick margarine
4	tablespoons cocoa
8	tablespoons half and half
1	box powdered sugar
1	teaspoon vanilla
1	cup chopped pecans, optional

To make icing, melt margarine, add cocoa and half and half and bring to a boil. Remove from heat and add powdered sugar, vanilla and pecans. Beat until smooth and spread over hot cake.

Vers

CHOCOLATE CHERRY CAKE

1	box chocolate cake mix
1	can cherry pie filling (raspberry is also good)
3	eggs
⅓	cup oil
1	teaspoon vanilla
	Whipping cream or frozen dairy topping

Mix all ingredients. Place in greased 9x13-inch pan and bake for 25 minutes at 350°. Top with thawed frozen dairy topping or whipped cream before serving.

GREAT AUNT GERTIE'S DUMP CAKE

1 21-ounce can cherry pie filling
1 8-ounce can crushed pineapple, undrained
1 box yellow cake mix
1 stick butter, cut in pieces
1 cup chopped walnuts, optional

Grease a 9x13-inch pan. Dump, in order, the cherries, undrained pineapple and dry cake mix, smoothing after each layer. Dot the butter on top. Do not mix. Sprinkle on the nuts. Bake 1 hour at 350°.

Serves 12

Vers

CHOCOLATE SHEET CAKE

2 cups flour
2 cups sugar
1 teaspoon baking soda
1 teaspoon cinnamon
1 stick butter or margarine
½ cup shortening
4 tablespoons cocoa
1 cup water
½ cup buttermilk
2 eggs
1 tablespoon vanilla

Sift dry ingredients together. In saucepan combine butter, shortening, cocoa and water and bring to a boil. Pour over sifted dry ingredients. Add buttermilk, eggs and vanilla. Beat well and pour into a buttered 9x12-inch pan. Bake at 400° for 25 minutes or until toothpick test comes out clean.

CHOCOLATE COCOA ICING

1 stick margarine
4 tablespoons cocoa
8 tablespoons half and half
1 box powdered sugar
1 teaspoon vanilla
1 cup chopped pecans, optional

For icing, melt margarine, cocoa and milk in a saucepan and bring to a boil. Add sugar, vanilla and pecans and beat well while still on the stove. Remove from heat and continue beating until smooth. Spread on cake while both are still hot.

4 DAY CAKE

1   box cake mix, any flavor and ingredients to prepare according to directions
¾   cup sugar
1   teaspoon vanilla
1   cup milk
1   8-ounce carton frozen dairy topping
1   cup coconut

Prepare cake according to directions on the package. Bake in a greased 9x13-inch baking dish. In a saucepan, combine sugar, vanilla and milk. Heat to dissolve sugar. When cake comes out of the oven, make holes in the cake with the tines of a large fork. Drizzle the warm milk mixture over the hot cake. When cake has cooled, ice with dairy topping and sprinkle coconut on top. Refrigerate 2 to 4 days before serving.

Eulalia Geisler

MILKY WAY CAKE

10   small Milky Way bars
1   stick butter
2   cups sugar
1   stick butter, softened
½   teaspoon butter flavoring
4   eggs
2½   cups flour
¼   teaspoon baking soda
¼   teaspoon salt
1   cup buttermilk
Powdered sugar

Melt Milky Way bars and butter, preferably in the top of a double boiler. In a mixing bowl combine the sugar, softened butter and butter flavoring. Add the eggs, one at a time, beating after each egg. Add alternately the flour, soda, salt and buttermilk. Slowly add the Milky Way mixture. Bake in a greased bundt pan for 1½ to 2 hours at 275°. Sprinkle powdered sugar on top when cake is partially cooled.

GERMAN SWEET CHOCOLATE CAKE

1	cup margarine
2	cups sugar
2½	cups flour, sifted
¼	teaspoon salt
1	teaspoon baking soda
4	egg separated
1	8-ounce bar German sweet chocolate melted
1	cup buttermilk
1	teaspoon vanilla

Cream margarine and sugar. Add egg yolks and melted chocolate. Add dry ingredients alternately with buttermilk. In a separate bowl, beat egg whites until stiff and then fold them into the batter. Pour batter evenly into 3 well-greased layer cake pans. Bake at 350° for 20 to 25 minutes. Allow to cool before icing.

COCONUT ICING

½	pint whipping cream
¼	pound butter
3	egg yolks
1	cup sugar
1	cup chopped pecans
1	cup shredded coconut

Icing: In a medium saucepan, combine cream, butter, egg yolks and sugar. Cook over medium heat about 12 minutes or until mixture begins to thicken. Remove from heat, add nuts and coconut, and allow to cool. When icing the cake, start with a generous amount of icing between the layers.

Vers

PEACH ALMOND JAM CAKE

1 cup butter, softened
2 cups sugar
4 eggs, separated
1 teaspoon almond extract
3 cups flour, sifted
½ teaspoon salt
3 teaspoons baking powder
1 cup half-and-half
2 cups peach jam

Cream butter and sugar. Add egg yolks, beating well after each addition. Stir in vanilla. In a separate bowl, sift together flour, salt and baking powder. Set aside. In another bowl, beat egg whites to form soft peaks. Gently add dry ingredients to butter mixture, alternating with half-and-half. Fold in egg whites. Divide into 3 well-greased and floured 8-inch cake pans. Bake at 350° for 30 minutes or until just done. Remove from oven, cool and remove from pans. Spread ½ cup of jam over each layer. Stack layers and ice.

BUTTER CREAM ICING

3 tablespoons butter or margarine, softened
1½ cups powdered sugar, sifted
2 tablespoons milk
1 teaspoon vanilla

In a mixing bowl, cream butter and powdered sugar. Add milk and vanilla. Ice cake.

This cake is good without icing.

PINEAPPLE DREAM CAKE

1   box white cake mix and ingredients to bake cake
1   cup sugar
1   20-ounce can crushed pineapple, drained
1   small box instant vanilla pudding and ingredients to prepare
1   cup sour cream
1   12-ounce carton frozen whipped topping, thawed
⅓   cup toasted coconut

Prepare cake according to directions on box. Bake in a well-greased 9x13-inch pan. While cake is cooling, heat sugar and pineapple in a small saucepan until sugar is dissolved. Pour this mixture over the cake. Prick the cake in several places with a toothpick to allow the liquid to seep into the cake. Prepare pudding as directed on the box. Add sour cream to the pudding and then refrigerate the mixture for about 15 minutes. Spread the pudding over the pineapple. Ice with whipped topping and then sprinkle with coconut. Refrigerate.

To toast coconut, preheat oven to 425°. Place coconut on a cookie sheet that has been lined with aluminum foil. Bake for 5 minutes or until the coconut is a golden brown. Watch the pan closely and shake or stir mixture once or twice to insure that it browns evenly.

APRICOT BRANDY POUND CAKE

3 cups sugar
2 sticks margarine
6 eggs
1 teaspoon vanilla
3 cups flour
¼ teaspoon baking soda
½ salt
1 cup sour cream
½ cup apricot brandy,
   Leroux brand preferred

Cream margarine and sugar. Add eggs, one at a time, beating well after each addition. Add flavoring. Sift flour, salt and soda. Add flour mixture to batter, alternating with sour cream and brandy. Pour batter into a well-greased tube pan. Bake at 325° for 1 hour and 10 minutes.

Grace DeuPree

BLUEBERRY POUND CAKE

1 8-ounce package cream cheese
½ cup oil
1 butter yellow cake mix
4 eggs
1 small box instant vanilla pudding
2 teaspoons vanilla
1 14-ounce can blueberries, rinsed and drained, or same amount fresh blueberries

Combine all ingredients. Place in a well-greased and floured bundt or tube pan. Bake at 350° for 45 to 50 minutes.

Raspberries or strawberries may be substituted for blueberries.

Gail Clark

BUTTERMILK POUND CAKE

6 eggs, separated
3 cups sugar
1 stick butter
½ cup solid shortening
3 cups flour
1 cup buttermilk
½ teaspoon salt
¼ teaspoon baking soda
3 teaspoons lemon, almond or orange extract

Blend sugar, butter and shortening. Add egg yolks, one at a time, and blend well. Add extract. Sift together dry ingredients and add alternately with buttermilk. Beat egg whites until not clear. Bake in a greased and floured tube pan for 1 hour 10 minutes at 350°.

Vers

CREAM CHEESE POUND CAKE

1 cup margarine, softened
½ cup butter, softened
1 8-ounce package cream cheese, softened
3 cups sugar
Dash of salt
2 teaspoons vanilla
6 large eggs
3 cups cake flour

Combine margarine, butter, cream cheese and sugar. Cream well. Add salt and vanilla. Add eggs one at a time, beating well after each addition. Add flour and beat well. Pour into a greased and floured bundt pan. Place in cold oven and set at 275°. Bake 1½ hours. Cool in pan before removing.

LEMON POUND CAKE

1   box yellow cake mix
1   small box lemon instant
    pudding
½   cup sugar
¾   cup oil
¾   cup water
4   eggs
1   8-ounce carton sour
    cream

Mix cake mix, pudding and sugar with a wooden spoon. Add oil and water and stir. Add eggs, one at a time, and beat with wooden spoon. Add sour cream. Bake in greased and floured tube pan at 350° for 50 to 60 minutes. Cool in pan 1 hour before removing.

Jeanne Edwards

SOUR CREAM POUND CAKE

6   eggs
3   cups sugar
3   cups flour
½   pound butter
½   pint sour cream
½   teaspoon baking soda
Pinch of salt
1   teaspoon almond
    extract

Cream butter and sugar. Add eggs one at a time, beating well after each egg. Add sour cream. Sift flour, soda and salt and add to mixture. Mix well. Add almond extract; mix. Grease and flour large bundt pan or tube pan. Pour in batter. Bake 1½ hours at 325°.

WHIPPING CREAM POUND CAKE

3 cups sugar
1 cup butter, softened
6 eggs
3 cups flour
1 teaspoon almond extract
1 cup whipping cream
Powdered sugar

Using an electric mixer, cream sugar and butter. Add eggs, one at a time, blending thoroughly after each addition. Add flour, almond extract, and whipping cream. Mix well. Grease and flour a tube or bundt pan. Pour batter in and put into a cold oven. Turn oven on to 325° and bake for 1 hour and 25 minutes. Remove from pan when cool. Dust with powdered sugar.

PUMPKIN CAKE

2 cups sugar
4 eggs
1½ cups salad oil
2 cups flour
1 teaspoon salt
2 teaspoons soda
3 tablespoons cinnamon
1½ cups pumpkin

Sift dry ingredients. Add eggs, oil and pumpkin. Blend and beat 1 minute. Pour into greased and floured bundt pan. Bake 1 hour at 350°. Allow to cool completely before icing.

ICING

½ box powdered sugar
½ stick butter
1 8-ounce package cream cheese
½ cup crushed pecans, optional
½ teaspoon vanilla

Blend icing ingredients and ice cooled cake.

PUMPKIN UPSIDE DOWN CAKE

3   large eggs, lightly beaten
2   15-ounce cans of pumpkin
1¼ cups sugar
1   12-ounce can evaporated milk
2   teaspoons cinnamon
1   teaspoon nutmeg
½   teaspoon ginger
1   package yellow cake mix
1½ sticks butter or margarine, melted
1   cup chopped pecans or walnuts, optional
Whipped cream, whipped

Preheat oven to 350°. Make filling by combining eggs, pumpkin, sugar, evaporated milk, cinnamon, nutmeg and ginger. Stir until well blended. Pour into ungreased 13x9x2-inch baking dish. Sprinkle dry cake mix evenly over filling. Drizzle melted butter evenly over cake mix. Bake 30 minutes. Remove from oven and sprinkle nuts on top. Return to oven and bake 30 minutes longer or until topping is golden brown. Serve with whipped cream.

Mom

STRAWBERRY CAKE

1   box yellow cake mix
1   3-ounce package strawberry Jell-O
1   cup oil
½   cup water
3   tablespoons flour
3   eggs
½   package frozen sliced strawberries, thawed

Mix cake mix and Jell-O together. Add oil, water, flour, eggs and strawberries. Mix until well blended. Bake in a large well-greased baking pan at 350° for 30 minutes. Allow cake to cool.

STRAWBERRY ICING

1   stick butter, softened
1   box powdered sugar
½   package frozen sliced strawberries, thawed

To prepare icing, mix softened butter, powdered sugar and strawberries. Beat until smooth and ice cooled cake.

RED VELVET CAKE

1 stick butter, softened
1½ cups sugar
2 eggs
1 2-ounce bottle red food coloring
1 tablespoon cocoa
2 cups flour
1 cup buttermilk
1 teaspoon salt
1 teaspoon vanilla
1 teaspoon baking soda dissolved in 1 tablespoon vinegar

Cream butter and sugar. Add eggs. Dissolve cocoa in food coloring and add to butter mixture. Alternately add flour and buttermilk. Mix well and then add salt, vanilla and dissolved baking soda. Grease and flour two 9-inch cake pans. Add batter evenly to both. Bake at 350° for 25 minutes or until done.

FROSTING

1 cup milk
¼ cup flour
Dash salt
1 cup sugar
1 stick margarine
1 stick butter
1 teaspoon vanilla

Frosting: Pour milk into a saucepan and whisk in the flour and salt. Cook over medium heat until thickened. Set aside and allow to cool. In a separate bowl, cream butter and sugar until fluffy. Add vanilla and then add this mixture to the cooled sauce. Stir together and then ice the cake.

Mom

BLUE GOO PIE

1½ cups frozen dairy topping, thawed
1 4-ounce package cream cheese, softened
1 cup sugar
2 bananas, thinly sliced
½ can blueberry pie filling

Blend first three ingredients with electric mixer until smooth. Line pie shell with bananas. Pour whipped cream mixture over bananas and top with pie filling. Use more pie filling if necessary. Chill before serving.

Mom

BUTTERMILK PIE

1	9-inch pie crust
1	cup sugar
3	tablespoons flour
3	eggs, beaten
4	tablespoons butter, melted and cooled
1	cup buttermilk
½	teaspoon vanilla extract
2	tablespoons lemon juice
1	tablespoon grated lemon zest
½	teaspoon grated nutmeg

Preheat oven to 425°. Cover pie crust snugly with foil and bake for 6 minutes. Remove foil and bake 4 more minutes. Mix sugar and flour. Beat in eggs, melted butter, buttermilk, vanilla, lemon juice and zest. Pour filling into cooled pie shell and bake 10 minutes then sprinkle with nutmeg. Lower oven temperature to 350° and bake 30 more minutes or until knife inserted in center comes out clean. Serve lukewarm, refrigerate leftover pie.

Kathy Daume

CARAMEL PIE

½	cup sugar
2	egg yolks
⅔	cup sugar
2	tablespoons flour
Dash of salt	
1½	cups milk
1	teaspoon vanilla
1	tablespoon butter, melted
1	9-inch pie shell, baked
Sweetened whipping cream, whipped	

Melt ½ cup of sugar until medium brown in color. In a mixing bowl, combine the egg yolks, ⅔ cup sugar, flour and salt until well blended. Add milk, vanilla and melted butter. Pour this mixture into the browned sugar and cook until thickened. Pour into the baked pie shell and allow to cool before serving. Top with sweetened whipped cream.

Vers

CHOCOLATE ICEBOX PIE

1½ sticks butter
1 cup sugar
3 eggs
3 cubes unsweetened chocolate, melted
1 teaspoon vanilla
1 9-inch graham cracker pie crust

WHIPPED CREAM TOPPING
1 cup whipping cream
1 teaspoon sugar
1 teaspoon vanilla
Chocolate shavings

Beat butter and sugar until creamy. Add eggs one at a time, beating mixture until fluffy after each egg is added. Add the melted chocolate and vanilla. Beat until fluffy. Pour into pie shell. Chill. Cover with whipped cream topping.

Topping: Pour whipping cream in mixer. Add sugar and vanilla and beat until thickened. Spread over chilled pie and top with chocolate shavings. Return to refrigerator until ready to serve.

Anne DeuPree Duke

CRANBERRY SURPRISE PIE

2 cups fresh cranberries
1½ cups sugar, divided use
½ cup chopped walnuts
2 eggs
1 cup flour
½ cup butter, melted
Ice cream or whipped cream

Rinse and gently pat dry cranberries. Spread cranberries over the bottom of a greased 10-inch pie plate. Sprinkle ½ cup sugar and walnuts over berries. In a separate bowl, beat eggs; add 1 cup sugar and cream well. Add flour and melted butter to egg mixture; beat well. Pour batter over cranberries and bake at 325° for 1 hour. Serve warm with ice cream or whipped cream on top.

Anne DeuPree Duke

CUSTARD PIE

3 eggs
1 13-ounce can
   evaporated milk
1 cup sugar
3 tablespoons flour
3 tablespoons butter,
   melted
½ teaspoon vanilla
Nutmeg to taste

Grease and flour a 9-inch glass pie plate. Combine all ingredients in a blender for 30 seconds. Pour into pie plate and bake at 350° for 40 to 45 minutes. Pie will rise, but will settle as it cools. Chill well.

BLUEBERRY-PEACH COBBLER

1 package blueberry
   muffin mix
½ cup sugar, divided use
1½ teaspoons cinnamon,
   divided use
6 tablespoons butter or
   margarine
½ cup chopped pecans,
   optional
2 cans peach pie filling
1 teaspoon almond
   extract
Vanilla ice cream

In a medium bowl combine dry muffin mix, ¼ cup sugar and ½ teaspoon cinnamon. Cut in butter and add nuts. Generously coat a 9x13-inch dish with cooking spray. In the baking dish, combine the pie filling, ¼ cup sugar, 1 teaspoon cinnamon, almond extract and the washed and drained blueberries. Spoon the crumb mixture over the peach mixture. Bake at 350° for 35 to 40 minutes or until topping is golden brown. Serve with ice cream.

Serves 12

Easy Fruit Cobbler

1	frozen fruit pie (peach, apple, etc.)
1	unbaked frozen pie crust
1½	cups sugar
1	cup butter
1-2	cups water

Crumble frozen pie and pie crust. Mix with sugar, butter, and water. Place in 9x13-inch baking dish. Bake at 350° for 1 hour.

Serves 10

Linda Mitchell

Key Lime Pie

1	9-inch pie crust, baked
4	egg yolks
6	egg whites
1	14-ounce can condensed milk
½	cup lime juice
¾	cup sugar
½	teaspoon cream of tartar

Beat egg yolks until lemon colored. Slowly blend in condensed milk. Add lime juice and mix well. In a separate bowl, combine egg whites and cream of tartar and beat until foamy. Continue beating adding sugar 1 tablespoon at a time until egg whites peak. Fold 6 tablespoons of the meringue into the filling. Pour into pre-baked pie shell. Top with meringue and bake at 325° until meringue is golden brown.

Lemon Pie

2	14-ounce cans sweetened condensed milk
1	egg
½	cup lemon juice
1	graham cracker pie crust
	Sweetened whipping cream, whipped

Blend first three ingredients and pour into pie crust. Refrigerate until set. Serve with whipped cream.

Diane Bifano

EASY LEMONADE PIE

1   8-inch graham cracker pie crust
1   6-ounce can frozen pink lemonade, thawed
2   tablespoons lemon juice
1   can Eagle Brand milk
1   4-ounce container frozen dairy topping, thawed

Mix lemonade, lemon juice and milk until slightly thickened. Fold in dairy topping and thoroughly blend. Put in pie crust and refrigerate for several hours before serving.

Sue Geren

MERINGUE PIE

3   egg whites, beaten stiff
1   teaspoon vanilla
1   cup sugar
½   teaspoon baking powder
¾   cup English walnuts or pecans
20 soda crackers, crumbled
Fruit
Sweetened whipping cream, whipped or ice cream

Mix all ingredients. Spray a large pie pan cooking spray and add mixture. Bake at 325° for 25 minutes. Chill. Cut like a pie and serve with fruit and whipped cream or ice cream.

Lucile Finch

PEACH COBBLER

½   stick butter
½   cup milk
½   cup flour
½   cup sugar
1   teaspoon baking powder
1   29-ounce can sliced peaches

Cut butter into small pieces and place in the bottom of a greased 2-quart rectangular baking dish. Mix flour, sugar, and baking powder. Stir in milk and mix until well blended. Pour into baking dish on top of butter. Spoon peaches into pan including juice. Bake at 350° for 1 hour. Serve warm.

GLAZED PEACH PIE

2½ cups fresh peach slices
1 tablespoon lemon juice
¼ cup sugar
1 8-inch unbaked pie shell
½ cup sugar
3 tablespoons cornstarch
2 tablespoons butter or margarine
⅛ teaspoon salt
⅛ teaspoon almond extract
Sweetened whipping cream, whipped

Drizzle lemon juice over peaches. Add ¼ cup sugar, mix and set aside for 1 hour. Bake pie shell according to package directions and allow to cool. Drain peaches, reserving syrup. Add enough water to the syrup to yield 1 cup. In a saucepan, blend ½ cup sugar and the cornstarch. Add reserve 1 cup of liquid and boil until thick and clear. Remove from heat and add butter, salt and extract. Stir in peaches and put in pie shell. Cool and top with whipped cream.

Mom

PECAN PIE

4 tablespoons butter, softened
½ cup brown sugar
1 cup dark corn syrup
1½ cups pecan halves
3 eggs
Pinch of salt
1 9-inch unbaked pie crust

Combine filling ingredients by beating together the butter and sugar. Stir in syrup. Add eggs one at a time, beating after each addition. Stir in 1 cup pecans and salt. Pour into pie shell and arrange remaining pecans on top. Bake at 350° for 45 minutes or until set and browned.

Vers

PUMPKIN CHIFFON PIE

1   cup canned pumpkin
½   cup cold milk
1   large package vanilla instant pudding
1   teaspoon pumpkin pie spice
3½   cups frozen whipped topping, thawed
1   graham cracker pie crust

Mix first five ingredients together reserving 1 cup of frozen topping. Place in pie shell. Freeze for at least 4 hours. Top with remaining topping before serving.

Marti Clinesmith

STRAWBERRY PIE

1   pint fresh strawberries, hulled and cut in half
1   9-inch baked pie crust
¼   cup cornstarch
¾   cup sugar
1   cup water
1   small box strawberry Jell-O
Frozen dairy topping

Mix and heat cornstarch, sugar and water stirring constantly until thickened. Add strawberry Jell-O. Cool. Add strawberries and pour into pie shell. Refrigerate until set. Cover with frozen dairy topping before serving.

Louise McCall

TOLL HOUSE PIE

2   eggs
½   cup all-purpose flour
½   cup sugar
½   cup brown sugar
1   cup butter, melted and
    cooled to room
    temperature
1   6-ounce package semi-
    sweet chocolate morsels
1   cup chopped walnuts,
    optional
1   9-inch deep-dish pie
    shell, unbaked
Sweetened whipping cream,
    whipped or ice cream

Preheat oven to 325°. In a large bowl, beat eggs until foamy. Add flour, sugar and brown sugar; beat until well blended. Blend in butter. Stir in morsels and walnuts. Pour into pie shell. Bake for 1 hour. Serve with whipped cream or ice cream.

CATHEDRAL WINDOW COOKIES

1   12-ounce package semi-
    sweet chocolate morsels
4   tablespoons butter
2   eggs, beaten
1   10.5-ounce package
    pastel-colored
    marshmallows
½   cup chopped pecans,
    optional
Powdered sugar

In a large saucepan, melt butter and chocolate. Remove from heat. Add eggs and stir thoroughly. Add marshmallows and pecans and mix well. Sprinkle powdered sugar on two sheets of wax paper. Place half of dough on each. Roll up dough in paper and shape to form logs. Refrigerate until firm and cut in slices before serving.

Mom

CHEESE BLINTZES

2 loaves thin sliced white bread
1 8-ounce package cream cheese, softened
2 egg yolks
½ cup sugar
½ pound butter, melted
Cinnamon sugar

Remove crusts from bread and roll each slice on both sides until very thin. Combine cream cheese, egg yolks and sugar. Spread each slice of bread with cream cheese mixture. Roll bread slices, dip each in melted butter and sprinkle with cinnamon sugar. Freeze blintzes. Bake at 350° for 10 minutes before serving.

Diane Bifano

CHOCOLATE CHIP COOKIES

1 cup butter or margarine, softened
¾ cup sugar
¾ cup brown sugar, packed
2 eggs
1 teaspoon vanilla
2¼ cups, sifted flour
1 teaspoon baking soda
1 teaspoon salt
1 12-ounce package semi-sweet chocolate chips
1 cup chopped nuts, optional

Cream together butter, sugars and vanilla until light and fluffy. Beat in eggs. Sift together dry ingredients and gradually add to creamed mixture until well blended. Fold in chocolate chips and nuts. Place teaspoonful amounts of batter onto ungreased cookie sheet (1 dozen per baking sheet) and bake at 350° for about 10 minutes or until lightly browned.

Makes about 5 to 6 dozen

CHOCOLATE CHIP SQUARES

½ cup butter, softened
¼ cup plus 2 tablespoons sugar
¼ cup plus 2 tablespoons brown sugar, packed
½ teaspoon vanilla
1 egg
1 cup flour
½ teaspoon baking soda
½ teaspoon salt
½ cup walnuts, optional
1 6-ounce package chocolate chips

Mix butter, sugar and vanilla. Beat in egg. Blend in powdered ingredients. Mix in nuts. Spread in greased baking pan. Sprinkle chocolate chips over batter. Bake at 350° for about one minute or until chocolate chips begin to melt. Remove from oven and swirl chips until marbleized. Continue baking for 12 to 14 minutes.

Marguerite Zack

SCOTCH SHORTBREAD

1 cup butter, softened
½ cup sugar
2½ cups sifted flour

Cream butter and add sugar. Add flour and mix well with hands. Divide dough into two layer cake pans. Bake at 300° for 20 minutes. Remove from oven and cut into small wedges. Return to oven until lightly browned.

Mom

BROWNIES

5	eggs, beaten
2½	cups sugar
1¼	cups flour
10	tablespoons margarine
4	squares Baker's semi-sweet chocolate
1	cup chopped pecans or walnuts, optional
2	teaspoons vanilla
Dash of salt	

Beat eggs and then add sugar and flour. Melt butter and chocolate and add to egg mixture. Add nuts, vanilla and salt. Bake at 350° for 20 to 25 minutes in 9x13-inch greased pan. After 10 minutes of baking, remove brownies from the oven and shake the pan until the batter falls. Continue baking. Sprinkle with powdered sugar while still hot.

Mom

LIGHT BROWNIES

1	stick butter
1	box light brown sugar
2	eggs
1½	cups flour
2	teaspoons baking powder
1	teaspoon vanilla
½	cup chopped pecans

Melt butter and brown sugar together and let cool. Add remaining ingredients and mix well. Bake at 350° for 10 minutes. Remove and shake pan. Continue baking about 10 minutes or until done.

Tess Latham

GOLDEN BROWNIES

1 package butter pecan cake mix
1 stick margarine, melted
1 egg
1 teaspoon vanilla
1 stick margarine, melted
1 8-ounce package cream cheese
2 eggs
1 box powdered sugar
1 teaspoon vanilla
1 cup chopped pecans, optional

Mix first four ingredients together and press into a 9x13-inch pan. Do not grease pan. Cream remaining ingredients and spread over cake mix. Top with 1 cup chopped pecans. Bake at 350° for 40 to 45 minutes at 350°.

CHESS SQUARES

1 box butter cake mix
1 stick butter, melted
3 eggs, beaten
1 8-ounce package cream cheese, softened
1 box powdered sugar

Mix cake mix, butter and 1 egg until well blended and spread into greased 13x9x2-inch Pyrex dish. Beat cream cheese, 2 eggs and powdered sugar and pour over dough. Bake at 350° for 30 minutes or until brown around the edges. Cut into squares like brownies.

Mom

LEMON SQUARES

1 cup butter
½ cup powdered sugar
2 cups flour
4 large eggs
2 cups granulated sugar
1 tablespoon flour
½ teaspoon baking powder
⅓ cup fresh lemon juice
1 cup chopped pecans, optional

Cream butter and powdered sugar. Gradually stir in 2 cups flour and beat well. Spread this mixture on the bottom of an ungreased 13x9x2-inch Pyrex baking dish. Bake at 325° for 15 minutes. Remove from oven. In a separate bowl, beat eggs slightly and add granulated sugar, 1 tablespoon flour, baking powder, lemon juice and nuts. Stir (do not beat) until well mixed. Pour over the warm crust. Return to 325° oven for about 45 minutes or until brown.

Vers

POOR MAN'S COOKIES

1 cup raisin
2 cups water
1 cup sugar
½ cup salad oil
1 egg
2 cups flour
1 teaspoon cinnamon
1 teaspoon baking soda

Place raisins in water and simmer until 1 cup of juice remains. Add all other ingredients and mix well. Place in a well-greased 9x13-inch pan. Bake at 350° for 30 minutes.

Aunt Helen

Edna's Banana Pudding

3 eggs, separated
1 cup plus 2 tablespoons sugar
3 heaping tablespoons of flour
Dash of salt
2½ cups milk
⅔ stick butter
2 teaspoon vanilla
4 medium bananas

Mix egg yolks with 1 cup sugar, flour, salt, milk, and ⅓ stick butter. Cook over medium heat, stirring constantly, until thick like pudding. Remove from heat and add other ⅓ stick of butter and 1 teaspoon of vanilla to hot mixture. Set aside to cool while beating egg whites for meringue. Add sugar and 1 teaspoon vanilla to whites and continue to beat until stiff. Pour pudding into bottom of well-greased casserole. Add vanilla wafers and then sliced bananas. Top with more wafers followed by meringue. Bake at 400° until golden brown. Watch pudding carefully in order not to let the meringue burn.

Edna Douglas

Easy Bananas Foster

4 tablespoons brown sugar
2 tablespoons butter
2 bananas
Cinnamon
Vanilla ice cream

Peel and slice bananas lengthwise. Melt butter and add sugar. Add bananas and sauté until tender. Sprinkle with cinnamon and serve warm over vanilla ice cream.

Serves 4

CAFÉ QUEBEC

1 cup strong coffee
24 marshmallows
1 cup whipping cream, whipped
Chocolate shavings

Heat the coffee and marshmallows until melted. Cool and then fold in whipped cream. Place in parfait or champagne glasses. Chill. When ready to serve, top each with whipped cream, chocolate shavings and a thin cookie or wafer.

Serves 8

Marti Clinesmith

BOILED CUSTARD

⅓ cup flour
1 cup sugar
1 quart whole milk
2 eggs
1 pint whipping cream, whipped
1 teaspoon vanilla
Pinch of salt

Mix well flour and sugar. Add milk a little at a time until mixture is smooth. Add eggs one at a time with a mixer or beater. Cook over low heat until mixture forms long strings and begins to thicken. Set aside until completely cooled. Fold in whipped cream, vanilla and salt.

Vers

ENGLISH TOFFEE DESSERT

¾ cup sugar
½ cup whipping cream
¼ cup light corn syrup
2 tablespoons butter
½ cup Heath bars, broken
2 pints fresh strawberries, hulled

In a medium saucepan, combine sugar, whipping cream, corn syrup and butter. Boil for 1 minute. Remove from heat, stir in candy and allow to cool. Serve over strawberries. Top with additional whipped cream if desired.

Serves 6 to 8

173

FRUIT BRÛLÉE

3   cups fruit (peaches,
     strawberries,
     blueberries, etc.)
1   cup sour cream
1   teaspoon vanilla
1   cup firmly packed
     brown sugar

Place fruit in a 9-inch glass pie pan. In a bowl, combine sour cream and vanilla. Pour over fruit. Sprinkle evenly with brown sugar. Broil until sugar caramelizes. Watch carefully - sugar should melt but not burn. Cover and refrigerate several hours.

Serves 4 to 6

PEANUT BUTTER FUDGE

3   cups sugar
¾   cup margarine
⅔   cup evaporated milk
1½   cups crunchy peanut
      butter
1   7-ounce jar
      marshmallow creme
1   teaspoon vanilla

Combine sugar, margarine and milk in a heavy 2½-quart saucepan; bring to a full rolling boil, stirring constantly. Continue boiling 5 minutes over medium heat, stirring constantly to prevent scorching. Remove from heat, add peanut butter and stir until melted. Add marshmallow creme and vanilla; beat until well

LEMON SPONGE

2 tablespoons butter, melted
1 cup sugar
¼ cup flour
⅛ teaspoon salt
5 tablespoons lemon juice
1 rind of lemon, grated
3 eggs, separated
1½ cups scalded milk

Cream butter with sugar, flour and salt. Add lemon juice and rind. Set aside. Beat egg yolks well. Beat a little scalded milk into egg yolks; then return egg mixture to milk, beating constantly. Add to creamed mixture and mix well. Fold in stiffly beaten egg whites. Pour into greased custard cups or a greased shallow baking dish, placed in a pan of hot water. Bake in preheated 350° oven for 45 minutes. When baked, each dessert will have custard on the bottom and sponge cake on top. Serve hot or cold.

Serves 8

Sue Geren

STRAWBERRIES ROMANOFF

1 quart sour cream
2 cups light brown sugar
Dash of nutmeg
Dash of cinnamon
1 teaspoon light rum, optional
Fresh strawberries

Thoroughly mix all ingredients and serve over fresh strawberries. Sauce will keep in the refrigerator for several days.

CHOCOLATE ICE CREAM

3 cans Eagle Brand milk
1 can Hershey's
   Chocolate sauce
1½ quarts milk

Mix Eagle Brand milk, chocolate sauce, and milk. Put in container or ice cream freezer and freeze.

Mary Lou Davis

PEACH ICE CREAM

6 large, very ripe peaches
1 cup sugar
4 eggs
3 cups sugar
2 quarts milk
1 quart whipping cream
1½ tablespoons vanilla

Peel, slice and mash peaches with potato masher. Stir in 1 cup sugar and set aside. Beat eggs in a large bowl; add sugar and mix well. Heat 1 quart of milk to scalding point and add to egg mixture, beating constantly. Pour into the freezer container and blend in the other quart of milk. Beat the whipping cream, not too stiff, and fold into the mixture in the container with the peaches and vanilla. Freeze in a large electric freezer.

HOMEMADE VANILLA ICE CREAM

2 cups sugar
6 eggs, beaten
1 14-ounce can condensed milk
2 13-ounce cans evaporated milk
2 quarts cream
2 tablespoons vanilla

Combine all ingredients mixing well. Pour into 1½ to 2 gallon freezer and freeze until firm.

WARM CINNAMON BERRY SAUCE

2 pints berries (raspberries, blueberries or blackberries)
5 tablespoons sugar
1 tablespoon lemon juice
1½ teaspoons cinnamon

Combine all ingredients in a saucepan and let sit for 5 minutes. Heat over medium heat until the berries have heated through, about 5 minutes. Remove berries with a slotted spoon. Bring the liquid to a boil and continue stirring until slightly thickened. Pour sauce back over the berries. Serve warm over ice cream, frozen yogurt or pound cake.

Makes 8 servings

Index

A

Acorn Squash, Baked 97
Adult Macaroni & Cheese 84
Almond Crusted Sole 137
Aloha Shrimp Salad 47
Anne's Cinnamon Rolls 70
APPETIZERS
  Almond Cheese Spread 18
  Artichoke & Shrimp Dip 8
  Artichoke Bacon Dip 19
  Artichoke Dip 8
  Artichoke Nibbles 8
  Bacon and Tomato Spread 20
  Bacon Bread 10
  Bacon Cheese Spread 20
  Black-Eyed Pea Dip 9
  Bob's Dip 10
  Broccoli Dip 12
  Cheese Ring 18
  Cheese Spread 20
  Chili Dip 11
  Chutney Cheese Spread 21
  Clam Dip 22
  Cold Artichoke Dip 19
  Cold Artichoke Spread 19
  Crab Dip 22
  Crab Tortilla Rollups 22
  Crab-Stuffed Mushrooms 13
  Crabmeat Dip 23
  Crabmeat Mornay Dip 12
  Curried Chutney Spread 21
  Deviled Eggs 24
  Easy Clam Dip 21
  Easy Guacamole 25
  Easy Stuffed Mushrooms 15
  Everyone's Favorite Dip 25
  French Bread Spread 11
  Fresh Shrimp Dip 28

  Green Chilie and Cheese Dip 25
  Hot Black-Eyed Pea Dip 9
  Hot Bread Snacks 10
  Hot Cheese Canapés 11
  Hot Crabmeat Cheese Puffs 13
  Hot Onion Dip 14
  Hot Parmesan Spinach Dip 17
  Jalapeño Cheese Squares 13
  Jalapeño Deviled Eggs 23
  Jalapeño Dip 24
  Louise's Shrimp Dip 29
  Mango Salsa 26
  Mexican Layer Dip 27
  Mexican Layer Dip II 27
  Mushroom Crescent Snacks 15
  Oyster Cracker Snack 28
  Parmesan Mustard
    Chicken Wings 16
  Party Pizzas 16
  Pineapple Salsa 26
  Quick Spinach Dip 30
  Shrimp Con Queso 14
  Shrimp Dip 29
  Spinach Artichoke Dip 17
  Spinach Dip 30
  Tangy Shrimp Dip 30
  Toasted Brie 9
  Tomato Toasties 18
Apple Breakfast Lasagna 54
Apple Buttermilk Cake 142
Apricot Brandy Pound Cake 153
Apricot Nectar Cake 142
Apricot-Pineapple Salad 39
ARTICHOKE(S)
  Artichoke & Shrimp Dip 8
  Artichoke and Rice Salad 42
  Artichoke Bacon Dip 19
  Artichoke Dip 8
  Artichoke Nibbles 8

Cold Artichoke Dip 19
Cold Artichoke Spread 19
Egg and Artichoke Casserole 57
Marinated Vegetable Salad 50
Spinach Artichoke Dip 17

ASPARAGUS
Asparagus Venetian 78
Cold Vegetable Salad 49
Easy Fresh Asparagus 78
Spring Salad 49

AVOCADO(S)
Avocado-Tomato Salad 40
Easy Guacamole 25
Everyone's Favorite Dip 25
Guatemalan Guacamole 24
Mexican Layer Dip 27
Mexican Layer Dip II 27
Regatta Salad 47

B

BACON
Artichoke Bacon Dip 19
Bacon & Egg Casserole 55
Bacon and Tomato Spread 20
Bacon Bread 10
Bacon Cheese Spread 20
Cheesy New Potatoes 89
Hearty Brunch Casserole 59
Overnight Egg Casserole 60
Tomato Toasties 18
Bailey's Chocolate
   Chip Cheesecake 143
Baked Acorn Squash 97
Baked Beans 79
Baked Chicken Breasts 115
Baked Eggplant 84
Baked Fish 138
Baked Potato Casserole 88
Baked Potato Soup 34
Baked Squash 98

BANANA(S)
Banana Bread 68
Banana Cake 144
Blue Goo Pie 158

Blueberry Banana Bread 68
Coconut Bananas 40
Easy Bananas Foster 172
Edna's Banana Pudding 172
Fruit Salad 40
Strawberry-Banana Bread 74
Barbecued Spare Ribs 130
Barley Bake, Piñon Nut 78
Basic Muffins 67
Basted Grilled Chicken 119
BBQ Shrimp and Grits 133

BEAN(S)
Baked Beans 79
Black Bean Potato Salad 46
Episcopal Green Beans 79
Garlic Green Beans 79
Green Bean Bundles 80
Marti's Green Beans 80

BEEF
Beef Stew 104
Beef Stroganoff 104
Beef Tenderloin 102
Betsy's Brisket 102
French Dip Sandwiches 107

Ground
Beef Casserole 103
Chili Dip 11
Country Pie 105
Enchilada Casserole 106
Hot Chili Soup 105
King Ranch Beef 108
Lasagna 108
Meat Loaf 109
Mexican Soup 35
Monterey Casserole 110
Nacho Casserole 109
Party Pizzas 16
Spaghetti Casserole 112
Spaghetti Pie 113
Spaghetti Sauce 114
Taco Meat 112
Mock Beef Bourguignonne 103
Pan Broiled Filet Mignon 107
Pot Roast 111
Shish Kabob Marinade 111

Steak Soup 37
Three Day Veggie Soup 38
Veal
    Veal Marsala 114
Beer Bread 67
Belgian Waffles 65
Betsy's Brisket 102
BEVERAGES
    Cranberry Punch 32
    Egg Nog 31
    Hot Chocolate Mix 31
    Irish Cream 32
    Spice Tea Mix 31
    Warm Holiday Punch 32
Black Bean Potato Salad 46
BLACK-EYED PEAS
    Black-Eyed Pea Dip 9
    Black-Eyed Pea Salad 42
    Chuck's Black-Eyed Peas 87
    Delicious Black-Eyed Peas 87
    Hot Black-Eyed Pea Dip 9
Blender Hollandaise 75
Blender Potatoes 89
Blue Goo Pie 158
BLUEBERRY
    Blue Goo Pie 158
    Blueberry Banana Bread 68
    Blueberry Jell-O Salad 41
    Blueberry Muffins 67
    Blueberry Pound Cake 153
    Blueberry Streusel 144
    Blueberry-Peach Cobbler 161
Bob's Dip 10
Boiled Custard 173
BREAD(S)
    Anne's Cinnamon Rolls 70
    Apple Breakfast Lasagna 54
    Bacon Bread 10
    Banana Bread 68
    Basic Muffins 67
    Beer Bread 67
    Belgian Waffles 65
    Blueberry Banana Bread 68
    Blueberry Muffins 67
    Broccoli Cornbread 69

Buttermilk Pancakes 66
Camille's Biscuits 68
Cinnamon Rolls 69
Coffee Cake 71
Custard French Toast 66
French Bread Spread 11
Garlic or Spinach Bread 72
Hot Bread Snacks 10
Mexican Cornbread 72
Poppy Seed Muffins 73
Pumpkin Bread 73
Sausage Rolls 61
Sausage Swirls 62
Strawberry Bread 74
Strawberry-Banana Bread 74
Waffles 65
Zucchini Bread 75
Breakfast Pizza 56
BROCCOLI
    Broccoli Casserole 81
    Broccoli Cheese Soup 34
    Broccoli Cornbread 69
    Broccoli Dip 12
    Cold Vegetable Salad 49
Broiled Fish 138
Brownies 169
Brownies, Golden 170
Brownies, Light 169
Brunch Casserole 54
Bunny's Shrimp 132
Buttermilk Pancakes 66
Buttermilk Pie 159
Buttermilk Pound Cake 154
Butterscotch Pudding Cake 145

C

CABBAGE
    Chinese Coleslaw 44
    Curried Coleslaw 44
    Sauerkraut Salad 45
Café Quebec 173
CAKE(S)
    4 Day Cake 149
    Apple Buttermilk Cake 142

Apricot Brandy Pound Cake 153
Apricot Nectar Cake 142
Bailey's Chocolate
    Chip Cheesecake 143
Banana Cake 144
Blueberry Pound Cake 153
Buttermilk Pound Cake 154
Butterscotch Pudding Cake 145
Carrot Cake 146
Chocolate Cake 147
Chocolate Cherry Cake 147
Chocolate Puddin' Cake 146
Chocolate Sheet Cake 148
Coffee Cake 71
Cream Cheese Pound Cake 154
German Sweet
    Chocolate Cake 150
Great Aunt Gertie's
    Dump Cake 148
Lemon Pound Cake 155
Milky Way Cake 149
Mississippi Mud Cake 145
Peach Almond Jam Cake 151
Pineapple Dream Cake 152
Pumpkin Cake 156
Pumpkin Upside Down Cake . 157
Red Velvet Cake 158
Sour Cream Pound Cake 155
Strawberry Cake 157
Whipping Cream
    Pound Cake 156
California Coleslaw 43
Camille's Biscuits 68
Candied Sweet Potatoes 91
Caramel Pie 159
Carrot Cake 146

CARROTS
Carrot Cake 146
Glazed Carrots 81
Cathedral Window Cookies 166

CAULIFLOWER
Company Cauliflower 80
Cerf Chicken 116
Charlotte's Sausage Casserole 56

CHEESE
Almond Cheese Spread 18
Bacon Cheese Spread 20
Bob's Dip 10
Broccoli Cheese Soup 34
Cheese Grits Soufflé 63
Cheese Onion Squares 85
Cheese Ring 18
Cheese Spread 20
Cheesy New Potatoes 89
Chili Dip 11
Chutney Cheese Spread 21
Cold Artichoke Dip 19
Company Eggs 55
Curried Chutney Spread 21
Douglass Ranch Chicken 118
French Bread Spread 11
Garlic Cheese Grits 64
Green Chili and
    Cheese Soufflé 58
Green Chilie and Cheese Dip 25
Hot Bread Snacks 10
Hot Cheese Canapés 11
Hot Crabmeat Cheese Puffs 13
Hot Parmesan Spinach Dip 17
Jalapeño Cheese Squares 13
Jalapeño Dip 24
Monterey Casserole 110
Pam's Breakfast Soufflé 60
Parmesan Mustard
    Chicken Wings 16
Shrimp Con Queso 14
Swiss Cheese and
    Egg Casserole 62
Swiss Cheese Soufflé 63
Toasted Brie 9
Cheese Blintzes 167
Cheesy Chicken Casserole 116
Cheesy New Potatoes 89
Chess Squares 170

CHICKEN
Baked Chicken Breasts 115
Basted Grilled Chicken 119
Cerf Chicken 116

Cheesy Chicken Casserole 116
Chicken & Rice 122
Chicken and Rice Salad 43
Chicken Casserole 115
Chicken Dijon 117
Chicken Shish Kabob 122
Chicken Spaghetti 124
Chicken Spaghetti #2 124
Cornish Game Hens 126
Countryside Chicken Bake 117
Douglass Ranch Chicken 118
Easy Chicken Tetrazzini 126
Friday Night
    Roasted Chicken 119
Honey Chicken 120
Imperial Chicken 120
One Dish Chicken 120
Overnight Chicken 121
Parmesan Mustard
    Chicken Wings 16
Poppy Seed Chicken 121
Regatta Salad 47
Simple Chicken 123
Simple Chicken #2 123
Spicy Chicken Spaghetti 125
Spinach Chicken Salad 48
Tortilla Soup 36
Ziploc Chicken 125
Chili Dip 11
Chili Soup, Hot 105
Chinese Coleslaw 44
Chinese Fried Rice 92

CHOCOLATE
Bailey's Chocolate
    Chip Cheesecake 143
Brownies 169
Cathedral Window Cookies 166
Chocolate Cake 147
Chocolate Cherry Cake 147
Chocolate Chip Cookies 167
Chocolate Chip Squares 168
Chocolate Ice Cream 176
Chocolate Icebox Pie 160
Chocolate Puddin' Cake 146

Chocolate Sheet Cake 148
German Sweet
    Chocolate Cake 150
Hot Chocolate Mix 31
Milky Way Cake 149
Mississippi Mud Cake 145
Toll House Pie 166
Chuck's Black-Eyed Peas 87
Chutney Cheese Spread 21
Cinnamon Rolls 69
Cinnamon Rolls, Anne's 70
Clam Dip 22
Clam Dip, Easy 21
Coconut Bananas 40
Coffee Cake 71
Cold Artichoke Dip 19
Cold Artichoke Spread 19
Cold Vegetable Salad 49
Company Cauliflower.................... 80
Company Eggs 55
Company Shrimp Casserole 134
COOKIES
    Brownies 169
    Cathedral Window Cookies 166
    Cheese Blintzes 167
    Chocolate Chip Cookies 167
    Golden Brownies 170
    Light Brownies 169
    Poor Man's Cookies 171
    Scotch Shortbread 168
CORN
    Corn Chowder 35
    Corn Pudding 82
    Donna's Corn Casserole 82
Cornbread, Broccoli 69
Cornbread Dressing 83
Cornbread, Mexican 72
Cornish Game Hens 126
Country Pie 105
Countryside Chicken Bake 117
CRABMEAT
    Crab Cakes 136
    Crab Dip 22
    Crab Tortilla Rollups 22

Crab-Stuffed Mushrooms 13
Crabmeat Dip 23
Crabmeat Mornay Dip 12
Deviled Crab 137
Hot Cheese Canapés 11
Hot Crabmeat Cheese Puffs 13
CRANBERRY
Cranberry Punch 32
Cranberry Surprise Pie 160
Quick Cranberry Salad 39
Warm Holiday Punch 32
Crawfish Cardinale 132
Cream Cheese Pound Cake 154
Creamed Onions 86
Creamed Spinach 94
Creamed Spinach Casserole 94
Curried Chutney Spread 21
Curried Coleslaw 44
Custard French Toast 66
Custard Pie 161

D

Delicious Black-Eyed Peas 87
DESSERTS
Blueberry Streusel 144
Blueberry-Peach Cobbler 161
Boiled Custard 173
Café Quebec 173
Cheese Blintzes 167
Chess Squares 170
Chocolate Chip Squares 168
Easy Bananas Foster 172
Easy Fruit Cobbler 162
Edna's Banana Pudding 172
English Toffee Dessert 173
Fruit Brûlée 174
Lemon Sponge 175
Lemon Squares 171
Peach Cobbler 163
Peanut Butter Fudge 174
Strawberries Romanoff 175
Warm Cinnamon
    Berry Sauce 177

Deviled Crab 137
Deviled Eggs 24
Dijon Pork Tenders 129
Donna's Corn Casserole 82
Douglass Ranch Chicken 118
Dressing, Cornbread 83

E

Easy Bananas Foster 172
Easy Chicken Tetrazzini 126
Easy Clam Dip 21
Easy Fresh Asparagus 78
Easy Fruit Cobbler 162
Easy Guacamole 25
Easy Hollandaise Sauce 75
Easy Lemonade Pie 163
Easy Stuffed Mushrooms 15
Edna's Banana Pudding 172
Egg Nog 31
Eggplant, Baked 84
EGG(S)
Bacon & Egg Casserole 55
Breakfast Pizza 56
Brunch Casserole 54
Charlotte's Sausage Casserole ..56
Company Eggs 55
Deviled Eggs 24
Egg and Artichoke Casserole 57
Green Chili and
    Cheese Soufflé 58
Ham & Egg Casserole 58
Hearty Brunch Casserole 59
Jalapeño Deviled Eggs 23
Mañana Casserole 59
Overnight Egg Casserole 60
Pam's Breakfast Soufflé 60
Sausage Casserole 61
Swiss Cheese and
    Egg Casserole 62
Enchilada Casserole 106
English Toffee Dessert 173
Episcopal Green Beans 79
Everyone's Favorite Dip 25

F

FISH

Almond Crusted Sole 137
Baked Fish 138
Broiled Fish 138
Fish Parmesan 139
Grilled Fish 139
French Bread Spread 11
French Dip Sandwiches 107
French Potato Salad 46
French Toast, Custard 66
Fresh Shrimp Dip 28
Friday Night Roasted Chicken ... 119
FRUIT (*See individual names*)
Fruit Brûlée 174
Fruit, Hot Curried 65
Fruit Salad 40
Fudge, Peanut Butter 174

G

GAME

Jake's Birds 127
Garlic Cheese Grits 64
Garlic Green Beans 79
Garlic or Spinach Bread 72
German Sweet Chocolate Cake ... 150
Glazed Carrots 81
Glazed Peach Pie 164
Golden Brownies 170
Great Aunt Gertie's
    Dump Cake 148
Green Bean Bundles 80
Green Beans, Episcopal 79
Green Beans, Garlic 79
Green Beans, Marti's 80
Green Chili and Cheese Soufflé 58
Green Chili Rice 92
Green Chilie and Cheese Dip 25
Grilled Fish 139
Grits, Garlic Cheese 64
Grits Soufflé, Cheese 63
Guatemalan Guacamole 24

H

Ham & Egg Casserole 58
Ham Loaf 127
Hash Brown Casserole 90
Hearty Brunch Casserole 59
Hollandaise, Blender 75
Hollandaise Sauce, Easy 75
Homemade Vanilla Ice Cream 177
Honey Chicken 120
Honey Mustard Dressing 51
Honey Mustard Pork Chops 128
Hot Black-Eyed Pea Dip 9
Hot Bread Snacks 10
Hot Cheese Canapés 11
Hot Chili Soup 105
Hot Chocolate Mix 31
Hot Crabmeat Cheese Puffs 13
Hot Curried Fruit 65
Hot Mustard 51
Hot Onion Dip 14
Hot Parmesan Spinach Dip 17

I

ICE CREAM

Chocolate Ice Cream 176
Homemade Vanilla Ice Cream 177
Peach Ice Cream 176
ICING
Brown Sugar
Butterscotch
    Pudding Cake 145
Butter Cream
Peach Almond Jam Cake 151
Chocolate
Mississippi Mud Cake 145
Chocolate Cocoa
Chocolate Cake 147
Coconut
German Sweet
    Chocolate Cake 150
Cream Cheese
Carrot Cake 146

Strawberry
   Strawberry Cake 157
Imperial Chicken 120
Irish Cream 32
Island Shrimp 135

J

Jake's Birds 127
Jalapeño Cheese Squares 13
Jalapeño Deviled Eggs 23
Jalapeño Dip 24
Jalapeño Spinach 95
Jezebel Sauce 51
Jill's Bermuda
   Jalapeño Macaroni Salad 45

K

Key Lime Pie 162
King Ranch Beef 108

L

Lasagna 108
LEMON
   Easy Lemonade Pie 163
   Lemon Pie 162
   Lemon Pound Cake 155
   Lemon Sponge 175
   Lemon Squares 171
Light Brownies 169
Louise's Shrimp Dip 29

M

Macaroni & Cheese, Adult 84
Make Ahead Mashed Potatoes 88
Mama Sue's Onion Casserole 85
Mañana Casserole 59
Mango Salsa 26
Marinated Pork Tenderloin 129
Marinated Pork Tenderloin #2 130
Marinated Vegetable Salad 50
Marti's Green Beans 80
Meat Loaf 109

Meringue Pie 163
Mexican Cornbread 72
Mexican Layer Dip 27
Mexican Layer Dip II 27
Mexican Soup 35
Milky Way Cake 149
Mississippi Mud Cake 145
Mock Beef Bourguignonne 103
Monterey Casserole 110
Muffins, Basic 67
Muffins, Blueberry 67
Muffins, Poppy Seed 73
MUSHROOM(S)
   Crab-Stuffed Mushrooms 13
   Easy Stuffed Mushrooms 15
   Mushroom Crescent Snacks 15
Mustard, Hot 51

N

Nacho Casserole 109

O

One Dish Chicken 120
Onion Glazed Pork Chops 128
ONION(S)
   Cheese Onion Squares 85
   Creamed Onions 86
   Hot Onion Dip 14
   Mama Sue's Onion Casserole ... 85
   Onion Casserole 84
   Onion-Roasted Potatoes 90
   Potatoes and Onions 89
Oriental Barbecued Shrimp 135
Overnight Chicken 121
Oyster Cracker Snack 28

P

Pam's Breakfast Soufflé 60
Pan Broiled Filet Mignon 107
Pancakes, Buttermilk 66
Parmesan Mustard
   Chicken Wings 16
Party Pizzas 16

PASTA
Adult Macaroni & Cheese 84
Chicken Spaghetti 124
Chicken Spaghetti #2 124
Easy Chicken Tetrazzini 126
Jill's Bermuda
    Jalapeño Macaroni Salad 45
King Ranch Beef 108
Lasagna 108
Spaghetti Casserole 112
Spaghetti Pie 113
Spaghetti Salad 48
Spicy Chicken Spaghetti 125

PEACH
Blueberry-Peach Cobbler 161
Peach Almond Jam Cake 151
Peach Cobbler 163
Peach Ice Cream 176
Peach Pie, Glazed 164
Peanut Butter Fudge 174
Pecan Pie 164
Perfect Rice 93

PIE(S)
Blue Goo Pie 158
Buttermilk Pie 159
Caramel Pie 159
Chocolate Icebox Pie 160
Cranberry Surprise Pie 160
Custard Pie 161
Easy Lemonade Pie 163
Glazed Peach Pie 164
Key Lime Pie 162
Lemon Pie 162
Meringue Pie 163
Pecan Pie 164
Pumpkin Chiffon Pie 165
Strawberry Pie 165
Toll House Pie 166

PINEAPPLE
Apricot-Pineapple Salad 39
Cranberry Punch 32
Fruit Salad 40
Pineapple Dream Cake 152
Pineapple Salsa 26

Scalloped Pineapple 64
Piñon Nut Barley Bake 78
Poor Man's Cookies 171
Poppy Seed Chicken 121
Poppy Seed Dressing 52
Poppy Seed Muffins 73

PORK (See also Sausage and Bacon)
Apple Breakfast Lasagna 54
Barbecued Spare Ribs 130
Dijon Pork Tenders 129
Ham & Egg Casserole 58
Ham Loaf 127
Honey Mustard Pork Chops 128
Marinated Pork Tenderloin 129
Marinated Pork
    Tenderloin #2 130
Onion Glazed Pork Chops 128
Pork Chops and Rice 129
Pot Roast 111

POTATO(ES)
Baked Potato Casserole 88
Baked Potato Soup 34
Black Bean Potato Salad 46
Blender Potatoes 89
Candied Sweet Potatoes 91
Cheesy New Potatoes 89
French Potato Salad 46
Hash Brown Casserole 90
Hearty Brunch Casserole 59
Instant Vichyssoise 38
Make Ahead Mashed Potatoes 88
Onion-Roasted Potatoes 90
Potatoes and Onions 89
Sweet Potato Soufflé 91

POULTRY (See Chicken)

PUMPKIN
Pumpkin Bread 73
Pumpkin Cake 156
Pumpkin Chiffon Pie 165
Pumpkin Upside Down Cake ... 157

Q

Quick Cranberry Salad 39
Quick Jalapeño Spinach 95

Quick Spinach Dip 30

R

Raspberry Salad 41
Red Velvet Cake 158
Regatta Salad 47
Rémoulade Sauce 52
RICE
  Artichoke and Rice Salad 42
  Chicken & Rice 122
  Chicken and Rice Salad 43
  Chicken Casserole 115
  Chinese Fried Rice 92
  Chuck's Black-Eyed Peas 87
  Company Shrimp Casserole 134
  Countryside Chicken Bake 117
  Green Chili Rice 92
  One Dish Chicken 120
  Perfect Rice 93
  Pork Chops and Rice 129
  Rice Casserole 93
  Rice O'Murphy 94
  Rice Pilaf 93
  Shrimp and Rice 131

S

SALAD
  Fruit
    Apricot-Pineapple Salad 39
    Blueberry Jell-O Salad 41
    Coconut Bananas 40
    Fruit Salad 40
    Quick Cranberry Salad 39
    Raspberry Salad 41
    Strawberry Salad 41
  Poultry
    Chicken and Rice Salad 43
    Regatta Salad 47
    Spinach Chicken Salad 48
  Seafood
    Aloha Shrimp Salad 47
  Vegetable
    Artichoke and Rice Salad 42
    Avocado-Tomato Salad 40

Black Bean Potato Salad 46
Black-Eyed Pea Salad 42
California Coleslaw 43
Chinese Coleslaw 44
Cold Vegetable Salad 49
Curried Coleslaw 44
French Potato Salad 46
Jill's Bermuda
  Jalapeño Macaroni Salad 45
Marinated Vegetable Salad 50
Sauerkraut Salad 45
Spaghetti Salad 48
Spring Salad 49
Tomato Aspic 50
SALAD DRESSING
  California Coleslaw 43
  Chicken and Rice Salad 43
  Cold Vegetable Salad 49
  Fruit
    Quick Cranberry Salad 39
  Honey Mustard Dressing 51
  Poppy Seed Dressing 52
  Regatta Salad 47
SAUCE
  Blender Hollandaise 75
  Dessert
    Apple Buttermilk Cake 142
    Easy Bananas Foster 172
    Strawberries Romanoff 175
    Warm Cinnamon
      Berry Sauce 177
  Easy Hollandaise Sauce 75
  Jezebel Sauce 51
  Rémoulade Sauce 52
Saucy Shrimp 136
Sauerkraut Salad 45
SAUSAGE
  Breakfast Pizza 56
  Brunch Casserole 54
  Charlotte's Sausage Casserole .. 56
  Chuck's Black-Eyed Peas 87
  Mañana Casserole 59
  Party Pizzas 16
  Sausage Casserole 61

Sausage Rolls 61
Sausage Swirls 62
SEAFOODS (*See Fish and individual names*)
Scalloped Pineapple 64
Scalloped Summer Squash 99
Scotch Shortbread 168
Shish Kabob Marinade 111
SHRIMP
  Aloha Shrimp Salad 47
  Artichoke & Shrimp Dip..............8
  BBQ Shrimp and Grits 133
  Bunny's Shrimp 132
  Company Shrimp Casserole 134
  Fresh Shrimp Dip 28
  Hot Cheese Canapés 11
  Island Shrimp 135
  Louise's Shrimp Dip 29
  Oriental Barbecued Shrimp 135
  Saucy Shrimp 136
  Shrimp and Rice 131
  Shrimp Bisque 36
  Shrimp Bread 131
  Shrimp Con Queso 14
  Shrimp Curry 134
  Shrimp Dip 29
  Shrimp Gumbo 37
  Shrimp/Crawfish Cardinale ...132
  Tangy Shrimp Dip 30
Simple Chicken 123
Simple Chicken #2 123
Sole, Almond Crusted 137
SOUP
  Baked Potato Soup 34
  Broccoli Cheese Soup 34
  Corn Chowder.............................35
  Hot Chili Soup 105
  Instant Vichyssoise 38
  Mexican Soup 35
  Shrimp Bisque 36
  Shrimp Gumbo 37
  Steak Soup 37
  Three Day Veggie Soup 38
  Tortilla Soup 36

Sour Cream Pound Cake 155
Spaghetti Casserole 112
Spaghetti Pie 113
Spaghetti Sauce 114
Spare Ribs, Barbecued 130
Spice Tea Mix 31
Spicy Chicken Spaghetti 125
SPINACH
  Creamed Spinach 94
  Creamed Spinach Casserole 94
  Garlic or Spinach Bread 72
  Hot Parmesan Spinach Dip 17
  Jalapeño Spinach 95
  Monterey Casserole 110
  Quick Jalapeño Spinach 95
  Quick Spinach Dip 30
  Spinach Artichoke Dip 17
  Spinach Casserole 95
  Spinach Chicken Salad 48
  Spinach Dip 30
  Spinach Soufflé 96
  Spinach Soufflé #2 96
  Spinach Soufflé #3 97
Spring Salad 49
SQUASH
  Baked Acorn Squash 97
  Baked Squash 98
  Scalloped Summer Squash 99
  Stuffed Squash.............................98
Steak Soup 37
Stew, Beef 104
STRAWBERRY(IES)
  English Toffee Dessert 173
  Strawberries Romanoff 175
  Strawberry Bread 74
  Strawberry Cake 157
  Strawberry Pie 165
  Strawberry Salad 41
  Strawberry-Banana Bread 74
Stroganoff, Beef 104
Stuffed Squash..............................98
Sweet Potato Soufflé 91
Sweet Potatoes, Candied 91
Swiss Cheese and Egg Casserole ..62
Swiss Cheese Soufflé 63

T

Taco Meat 112
Tangy Shrimp Dip 30
Tenderloin, Beef 102
Three Day Veggie Soup 38
Toasted Brie 9
Toll House Pie 166
Tomato Aspic 50
Tomato Tart 100
Tomato Toasties 18
TOMATO(ES)
   Avocado-Tomato Salad 40
   Bacon and Tomato Spread 20
   Tomato Aspic 50
   Tomato Tart 100
   Tomato Toasties 18
Tortilla Soup 36

V

Veal Marsala 114
VEGETABLES *(See individual names)*
Vichyssoise, Instant 38

W

Waffles, Belgian 65
Waffles 65
Warm Cinnamon Berry Sauce 177
Warm Holiday Punch 32
Whipping Cream Pound Cake 156

Z

Ziploc Chicken 125
ZUCCHINI
   Zucchini Bread 75
   Zucchini Soufflé 99

A CERF IN THE KITCHEN
8409 Pickwick Ln. #182
Dallas, Texas 75225-5323

Please send _____ copy(ies) of *For My Boys* @ $14.95 each _____

Postage and handling @ $ 3.00 each _____

Texas residents add sales tax @ $ 1.23 each _____

TOTAL _____

Name _____

Address _____

City _____ State _____ Zip _____

Make checks payable to *A Cerf in the Kitchen.*

A CERF IN THE KITCHEN
8409 Pickwick Ln. #182
Dallas, Texas 75225-5323

Please send _____ copy(ies) of *For My Boys* @ $14.95 each _____

Postage and handling @ $ 3.00 each _____

Texas residents add sales tax @ $ 1.23 each _____

TOTAL _____

Name _____

Address _____

City _____ State _____ Zip _____

Make checks payable to *A Cerf in the Kitchen.*

A CERF IN THE KITCHEN
8409 Pickwick Ln. #182
Dallas, Texas 75225-5323

Please send _____ copy(ies) of *For My Boys* @ $14.95 each _____

Postage and handling @ $ 3.00 each _____

Texas residents add sales tax @ $ 1.23 each _____

TOTAL _____

Name _____

Address _____

City _____ State _____ Zip _____

Make checks payable to *A Cerf in the Kitchen.*